A MANUAL FOR THE YOUNG

A MANUAL FOR THE YOUNG

A CLASSIC EXPOSITION OF PROVERBS 1-9

AND

AN ADDRESS TO YOUNG PERSONS

AFTER CONFIRMATION

CHARLES BRIDGES

SOLID GROUND CHRISTIAN BOOKS
BIRMINGHAM, ALABAMA USA

Solid Ground Christian Books
2090 Columbiana Rd, Suite 2000
Birmingham, AL 35216
205-443-0311
sgcb@charter.net
http://solid-ground-books.com

A Manual for the Young

Charles Bridges (1794-1869)

Proverbs first published in 1846
A Manual for the Young first published in 1859
An Address to Young Persons After Confirmation published in 1853

Solid Ground Classic Reprints

First printing of new edition November 2005

Cover work by Borgo Design, Tuscaloosa, AL
Contact them at nelbrown@comcast.net

*Special thanks to Ric Ergenbright for permission to use
the image on the cover. Visit him at ricergenbright.org*

ISBN: 1-59925-028-4

TABLE OF CONTENTS

INTRODUCTION TO NEW EDITION

A Manual for the Young has been a long time coming. I am not sure when I first noticed the note at the bottom of page xv of Bridges *On Proverbs,* but it was over ten years ago. It is there we are alerted to the fact that the author of the Commentary had been urged to publish the first nine chapters of his work and send it out as a MANUAL FOR THE YOUNG. Finally, at long last, you hold in your hands a book calculated to alter the course of history. These are bolds words, but I am convinced they are true words.

It is over 15 years since the Lord enabled me to bring back into print a little book called *Thoughts for Young Men* by J.C. Ryle. Within months 10,000 copies were scattered all over the world. Numerous letters arrived from the ends of the earth testifying of the powerful changes the Lord wrought in men's lives through this little book. *A Manual for the Young* is a book poised to perform the same work in the hearts of young men and women in the twenty-first century.

This little book has the potential of transforming lives because it is filled with Scripture. Not only is the vast majority of this book an exposition of the first nine chapters of Proverbs, but the last dozen pages, entitled *An Address to Young Persons After Confirmation* is packed with quotes from the Scriptures. Over 70 footnotes contain nearly 100 passages from the Word of God, all selected because of their fitness to speak to the hearts and consciences of the young.

I both invite you and challenge you as you prepare to read this book. Bridges will take you by the hand and lead you to the still waters and green pastures, but *you* must make the effort to drink and eat for yourself. Determine to come with a mind open to receive comfort, exhortation and rebuke. We would love to hear from you if you find this book helpful.

Michael Gaydosh
October 2005

PREFACE.

PROVERBIAL teaching is one of the most ancient forms of instruction. It was well adapted to the rudeness and simplicity of the first ages, when books were few, and philosophy little understood. The mind, unpractised to the slow process of reasoning, would be much more easily arrested by terse sentences, expressing a striking sentiment in the fewest words. The wise man himself has given the best definition of these sententious maxims. Their elegance he describes under the figure of "apples of gold in pictures (network) of silver."* Their force and permanent impression are "as goads and nails fastened by the Master of assemblies"† — driven closely home to the heart and conscience, and fastened in the memories by the appointed instructor of the people.

The antiquity of this teaching was recognised in the Church even before the age of Solomon. (1 Sam. xxiv. 13.) Classic Annals have recorded Aphorisms similarly constructed from men of wisdom. All of these however were of a later date. Some possibly might be dim scintillations from this fountain light; so that the King of Israel was — as an old expositor has remarked — 'the disciple of none, but the instructor of them all.'‡ Indeed his mind largely dealt in this intel-

---

* Chap. xxxv. 11. This image reminds us of Mr. Addison's apt description conceived in his best style of taste and beauty—'By similitudes, drawn from the visible parts of nature, a truth in the understanding is, as it were, reflected by the imagination. We are enabled to see something like colour and shape in a notion, and to discover a scheme of thoughts traced out upon matter. And here the mind receives a great deal of satisfaction, and has two of its faculties gratified at the same time, while the fancy is busy in copying after the understanding, and transcribing ideas out of the intellectual world into the material.' Concluding paper on 'the Pleasures of the Imagination.' *Spectator*, No. 421.

† Eccles. xii. 11. LXX. write παροιμιαι (παρα οιμος — via — sayings spoken in the way. Comp. Dr. Johnson's definition) a word often used in the New Testament for parables. (John, x. 6; xvi. 25, 29.) Marg. Both were of the same popular character. A proverb is often given in the form of a parable.

‡ Lavater. Comment. in Prov. Pref. Tigur. 1596.

lectual exercise. " He spake three thousand proverbs." (1 Kings, iv. 32.) And from this valuable mass of thought he was directed, under Divine inspiration, to " set in order" a collection for the instruction of the Church to the end of time.*

Possibly some would rather have desired the preservation of his discourses on Natural History (Ib. iv. 33), than on Practical Wisdom. But this Sovereign discrimination shews the real intent of the Scriptures — not to teach philosophy, but religion; not to make men of science, but men of sound godliness.

All competent judges will admit this Book to be eminently fitted for this great end. What the Roman Orator pronounced of Thucydides, applies far more truly to this King of Jerusalem — ' so full of matter, that he comprised as many sentences as words.'† This wonderful Book is indeed a mine of Divine wisdom. The views of God are holy and reverential. The observation of human nature is minute and accurate. The rule of life and conduct is closely applied, to make " the man of God perfect, thoroughly furnished unto all good works" (2 Tim. iii. 16, 17) ; so that, as Mr. Scott well remarks — ' we shall perceive the meaning and utility of the Proverbs, in proportion to our experience in true religion, our acquaintance with our own hearts, and with human nature, and the extent and accuracy of our observation on the character and affairs of men.'‡ Eusebius mentions the whole consent of the ancients, considering the Book of Proverbs to be ' Wisdom fraught with every kind of virtue.'§ Bishop Hall drew out mainly from it a complete system of ' Divine Arts.'‖ And though the Apostate Julian

---

* Eccles. xii. 9. Grotius supposes the Book to be a compilation from preceding writers. This degradation of Solomon is a gratuitous conjecture, unsupported by a tittle of evidence. But such are the irreverent liberties that proud learning dares to take with the Word of God !

† *Cicero de Oratore*, lib. ii. 14. Elsewhere he gives nearly the same judgment of Euripides. *Epist.* lib. xvi. 8.

‡ Pref. to Comment. on Prov.

§ Hist. lib. iv. c. 25. πανάρετον σοφίαν. Jerome's direction to one of his friends for the education of his daughter is — ' Let her have first of all the Book of Psalms for holiness of heart, and be instructed in the Proverbs of Solomon for her godly life.'—*Epist.* vii. *ad Lætam*. Matthew Henry, in his beautiful portrait of his mother, describes her as one, that was ' very well versed in Solomon's Proverbs, and the rules of wisdom, which may be fetched from thence for the conduct of human life, and knew how to apply them, and to use knowledge aright.'—*Sermon on the Death of Mrs. Katherine Henry.*

‖ ' Solomon's Divine Arts of Ethics, Politics, Economics — that is — the Government of Behaviour, Commonwealth, Family — drawn into method out of his Proverbs, and Ecclesiastes.' *Works*, viii. 427. Edited by Rev. P. Hall. Oxford, 1837.

scornfully preferred to it the sayings of Heathen Philosophy;* yet the apostrophe of the son of Sirach was justly applied to its author—'How wise wast thou in thy youth, and as a flood filled with understanding! Thy soul covered the whole earth, and thou fillest it with dark parables.'†

As to its 'canonical authority'—Michaelis well observes, 'that no Book of the Old Testament is so well ratified by the evidence of quotations.'‡ A few of the Jewish Talmudists appear to have expressed some doubt of its Divine stamp, but upon grounds so futile, that they were abandoned upon a more mature consideration.§ Ecclesiastical History has recorded only one dissentient from the judgment of the universal Church; and that one condemned by her authoritative council.‖ Witsius has admirably refuted the neological cavils of his day.¶ Nothing has been said from any quarter to weaken the unhesitating decision of our judgment, that the pen is that of the King of Israel; but the words are the wisdom of God.

Some difference exists among expositors as to the exact divisions of the Book. We have been led to divide it into three parts. In giving a more succinct account of these several parts, we shall avail ourselves largely, though necessarily in an abridged form, of the observations of a Biblical scholar, not more remarkable for his profound learning, than for his elegant taste.**

The first Part—all agree—extends from the opening of the Work to the close of the ninth chapter. It is—as Dr. Good observes—'chiefly confined to the conduct of early life. All the most formidable

---

* Apud Cyrill. Contra Julian. lib. vii.

† Ecclus. xlvii. 14, 15. The whole passage (verses 12–22) is very beautiful. Eusebius remarks of Solomon, that while, inspired by Divine wisdom, he consecrated all his writings to the profit and salvation of souls; yet he used these dark 'parables' for the exercise of the mind. *Contr. Marcell.* lib. i. c. iii. p. 17.

‡ Introd. to New Test. i. 207. Comp. especially in LXX. Chap. iii. 7, with Rom. xii. 16; 11, 12, with Heb. xii. 5, 6; 34, with James, iv. 6. 1 Pet. v. 5; x. 12, with 1 Pet. iv. 8; xi. 31, with 1 Pet. iv. 18; xxv. 6, 7, with Luke, xiv. 8–10; 21, 22, with Rom. xii. 20; xxvi. 11, with 2 Pet. ii. 22; xxvii. 1, with James, iv. 13, 14. It is a marked distinction drawn between this Book and the Apocryphal Book of Wisdom, so similar in character; that from the latter no quotation can be adduced in the New Testament.

§ Hottinger, Thesaur. Philol. lib. ii. c. 1. sect. 14. Comp. Carpzov. Introd. ad Lib. Canon. Part. ii. c. iv. § 7.

‖ Theodore Mopsuest. condemned by 5th Council of Constantinople, A.D. 551.

¶ Miscell. Sacra, lib. i. c. xviii. 30–34.

** Extracts from an unpublished Translation of the Book of Proverbs, by the late Dr. Good, in his *Life* by Dr. Gregory, pp. 286–306.

dangers to which this season is exposed, and "the sins which most easily beset it," are painted with the hand of a master. And while the progress and issues of vice are exhibited under a variety of the most striking delineations and metaphors, in their utmost deformity and horror ; all the beauties of language, and all the force of eloquence are poured forth in the diversified form of earnest expostulation, insinuating tenderness, captivating argument, and sublime allegory, to win the ingenuous youth to virtue and piety, and to fix him in a steady pursuit of his duties towards God and man. Virtue is pronounced in the very outset to be essential wisdom, and vice or wickedness essential folly. The only wise man therefore is declared to be the truly good and virtuous, or he that fears God, and reverences his law ; while the man of vice and wickedness is a fool, a stubborn or perverse wretch, and an abomination to Jehovah.

Wisdom is hence allegorized as a tree of life, yielding delicious shade, fruit, and protection to those that approach her branches ; throwing a garland of honour around their shoulders, and decorating their heads with a graceful chaplet, more precious than rubies. She is a sage and eloquent monitor, lifting up her warning voice at the gates and in the squares of the city ; denouncing to the young the snares and dangers, to which they are exposed ; and exhorting them to abandon "the way of the wicked, which is as darkness," for the path of the just, which is

> ———'As the brightening dawn,
> Advancing and brightening to perfect day.'*

The Second Part commences at the opening of the tenth chapter, as is obvious from the introductory clause. The style and manner of the second part are as different as possible from those of the first.

---

* We add two interesting testimonies, of a widely different character. 'The first part, including the first nine chapters, is a kind of exordium, and is varied, elegant, sublime, and truly poetical. The natural order is generally observed, and the parts are aptly connected together. It is embellished with very beautiful descriptions and prosopopœias, and adorned with the most finished style, together with every kind of poetical ornament ; so that it scarcely yields, in beauty, to any specimen of Sacred Poetry '—Bp. LOWTH'S *Lectures on Heb. Poetry*, **xxiv.** (Mr. Holden ventures to doubt whether this picture is not somewhat over-wrought.—*Pref. to Translation of Proverbs*, **xxxix.**) 'The first nine chapters of the Book of Proverbs present us with a most interesting specimen of "acceptable words." There is in them an inimitable union of admonitory fidelity, and enticing and subduing kindness. Like Paul, he "exhorts, comforts, and charges, as a father doth his children." The whole soul of the writer is breathed out in the earnestness of benevolent desire.'—WARDLAW *on Eccles.* **xii.** 10.

It is evidently designed for the use of persons advanced from the state of youth to that of manhood. While in the preceding, addressed to the young, the richest ornaments of the fancy are made choice of to captivate their attention, and allure them to a right practice ; in the present all is business and activity, brevity, continuity, and terseness. Every thought, though as highly polished, is at the same time as compressed as possible ; and the Writer, thoroughly aware of the value of every moment of time at this important period, lays down a complete series of short rules of life, and concentrates the most momentous precepts into the narrowest compass. The former appeals to the imagination ; the latter to the judgment. The one exhibits all the genius of poetry ; the latter all the art of composition ; and hence the general matter is rendered as attractive in the one instance as in the other.

'The great object in each of the Proverbs of the present part, is to enforce a moral principle in words so few, that they may be easily learnt, and so curiously selected and arranged, that they may strike and fix the attention instantaneously ; while, to prevent the mind from becoming fatigued by a long series of detached sentences, they are perpetually diversified by the changes of style and figure. Sometimes the style is rendered striking by its peculiar simplicity, or the familiarity of its illustration ;[1] sometimes by the grandeur or loftiness of the simile employed on the occasion ;[2] sometimes by an enigmatical obscurity,[3] which rouses the curiosity ; very frequently by a strong and catching antithesis ;[4] occasionally by a playful iteration of the same word ;[5] and in numerous instances by the elegant pleonasms or the expansion of a single or common idea by a luxuriance of agreeable words.'[6]

The Third Part we conceive to comprise the last seven chapters. The first five were written by Solomon, and edited some centuries after by the royal scribes in the reign of Hezekiah. The two last were written by separate hands, but preserved by Divine care, and altogether worthy of the place they hold in the inspired Canon.

The time when this book was written is a matter of some un-

[1] Chap. x. 19 ; xvi. 3 ; xxii. 2.
[2] Chap. xii. 58 ; xv. 11 ; xxi. 16, 22.
[3] Chap. xvi. 24 ; xvii. 8 ; xviii. 20.
[4] Chap. xiv. 10 ; xvi. 16 ; xvii. 10 ; xviii. 4 ; xix. 12 ; xx. 14.
[5] Chap. xi. 15 ; xiii. 20 ; xvii. 13, 15.
[6] Chap. xvi. 32 ; xvii. 17, 27, 28 ; xix. 6.

certainty. We cannot doubt but its contents were a part of "the three thousand Proverbs," which "he spake" before his most lamentable fall. (1 Kings, iv. 32.) They were therefore the exercise of his vast and comprehensive mind, under the full influence of his Divine wisdom. (Ib. verse 29.) They might, however, as many judicious critics have thought, have been "set in order" (Eccles. xii. 9) in their present form at a period subsequent to that afflictive event. Both parts of this hypothesis read a most solemn practical lesson. Do we see "outlandish women causing him to sin" (Neh. xiii. 26)—this "beloved of his God" falling himself into the snare, which he so minutely described, and against which he so earnestly and repeatedly warned?[1] Christian Ministers! does not Solomon, no less than St. Paul,[2] awfully teach us, that preaching to others will not save our own souls? The supposition of the posterior arrangement gives additional weight to his faithful admonitions. They come to us, like the exhortations of the restored Apostle,[3] with all the force of painful experience, in the true spirit of his Master's command—"When thou art converted, strengthen thy brethren."[4]

The interpretation of this Book requires much care and sobriety. Believing the principles of the Old and New Testament to be essentially the same, it seems reasonable to expound the more obscure by the more clear. The primary duty is indeed to affix to each Proverb its own literal and precise meaning. This is undoubtedly its spiritual meaning—that is—the mind of the Spirit. In an extended application of this discovered meaning, or in deducing inferences from it, judgment, not imagination, must be the interpreter. When no other than a literal meaning is plainly intended, the object must be, not to search out a new and miscalled spiritual meaning, but to draw practical instruction from its obvious sense.

There is, however—we may remark—a line to be drawn between exposition and illustration. The figures used in this Book, *after their literal meaning has been wrought out*, may fairly be used as illustrative of other collateral truths, not specifically intended. The Sacred Writers appear to warrant this principle of accommodation,[*] though

---

[1] Chap. ii. v. vii. ix. xxii. 14 ; xxiii. 27, 29.   [2] 1 Cor. ix. 27.
[3] 1 Pet. i. 13, 17 ; iv. 7 ; v. 8, with Matt. xxvi. 35.   [4] Luke, xxii. 32.
[*] See the Apostle's application of Ps. xix. 4, at Rom. x. 18, and DODDRIDGE's and GUYSE's *Paraphrase.* Comp. SCOTT *on Chap.* xxv. 6, 7.

its use requires great delicacy and consideration ; lest it should divest Scripture of its determinate meaning, and identify us with those artists, whom Dr. South memorializes, ' who can draw anything out of anything.'*

But with all care to preserve a soundly-disciplined interpretation, we must not forget, that the Book of Proverbs is a part of the volume entitled—" The word of Christ." (Col. iii. 16.) And so accurately does the title describe the Book, that the study of it brings the whole substance of the volume before us. It furnishes indeed the stimulating motive to search the Old Testament Scripture (John, v. 39)—the true key that opens the Divine Treasure-house ; so that, as Mr. Cecil observes—' If we do not see the golden thread through all the Bible, marking out Christ, we read the Scripture without the Key.'† This remark however does not undervalue its large mass of historical and practical instruction. But unquestionably Christ is the Sun of the whole Scripture system ; " and in his light we see the light" (Ps. xxxvi. 9), that reflects upon every point of practical obligation, and quickens life and energy throughout the whole Christian path. There is therefore, as Professor Franke reminds us—' much joy, comfort, and delight to be found in the writings of the Old Testament (especially in reading those places, which before were wearisome and almost irksome) when we perceive Christ is so sweetly pictured there.'‡

It has been recorded of Mary Jane Graham, ' that she was delighted in the course of her study of the Book of Proverbs to have Christ so much and so frequently before her mind'[1]—a recollection—her biographer ventured to observe—of ' great moment for the spiritual discernment of the divine wisdom treasured up in this storehouse of practical instruction.'§ Indeed, considering that these " Proverbs set in order—these words of the wise"—were originally " given from one Shepherd" (Eccles. xii. 9–11), whom we cannot surely fail to identify, we might naturally expect them to record distinct testimony of himself.

We cannot but fear, however, that this portion of the sacred volume

[1] Chap. i. viii. ix. &c.

* *Sermon on Matt.* v. 44.
† Mrs. HAWKES's *Life*, p. 171. So Augustine—'The Old Testament has no true relish if Christ be not understood in it.' *Ninth Tractat. on John.*
‡ *Christ the Sum and Substance of Holy Scripture.* Sect. xxi.
§ *Life,* chap. v.

is not generally estimated at its just value. Doubtless its pervading character is not, either *explicit* statement of doctrinal truth, or lively exercises of Christian experience. Hence the superficial reader passes over to some (in his view) richer portion of the Scriptural field. Now we readily admit, that all parts of the Bible are not of equal importance. But to value one part to the disparagement of another, is a slight to the divine testimony, that will be visited with a severe rebuke. Such a reader will only be possessed of mutilated fragments of truth, severed from their vital influence. He will never rise beyond a sickly sentimentalism. Seeking for novelty and excitement, rather than for the food of solid instruction; like Pharaoh's kine,* he devours much, but digests nothing. Never will he have light enough for the firm settlement of his faith; neither can he receive the true moulding of the mind of the Spirit, or the impress of the divine image.

But the question has been often asked—and that—not in cavilling, but in an anxiously enquiring, spirit—'How can I read this Book profitably?' Not unfrequently the confession has been added—'My mind and soul do not get food from it. I think I am less interested in this, than in any other, part of Scripture. I acknowledge the wisdom of its sayings. I am fully persuaded, that, being the Word of God, it was not written in vain. The fault therefore must be in myself. Still the question returns—How am I to read it with profit?'

Now it might almost appear, as if the rules given at the opening of the Book were intended to answer this question. (Chap. ii. 1–4.) Certain it is, that they do furnish the most satisfactory reply. The first and chief direction—that which gives life to every other—that which applies to every page and every verse of the Bible is—Begin with prayer—"Cry—lift up thy voice." Then combine a pondering mind with a praying heart. Actively apply thyself to "seek and search for the hid treasures." The riches lie not on the surface. Only those therefore, that dig into the bowels of the earth—not the readers, but " the *searchers of the Scriptures* "—are enriched. (John, v. 39.) If the surface be barren, the mine beneath is inexhaustible. Indeed it is a wise discipline, that has made an active spirit of meditation necessary to give solid and fruitful interest to this study, and to possess ourselves of

* Gen. xli. 20, 21. Comp. the picture drawn, 2 Tim. iii. 7.

a blessing, which carelessness or indolence will never realize. The promise here held out to diligent investigation fixed that intelligent Christian just mentioned ' on one occasion in intense meditation for two hours. She appeared to be lost in astonishment and gratitude at the condescension and kindness of God in giving a promise, so free, so encouraging. She grasped it, as if determined not to let it go.'°

The habit of interested attention being fixed, how shall we best " apply the heart to the understanding" of the Book? Here the valuable exercise of Scripture reference will greatly expand our own thoughtful meditation. Gather contributions from all parts of the field. Many a doubtful or apparently uninteresting Proverb will thus be brightened in instructive application. We are persuaded, that an enlarged Scriptural study, with whatever collateral helps may be within our reach, will bring no regret in having rested awhile in this part of the field, instead of passing onwards to a more inviting surface. To advert once more to our Scriptural student—' She frequently employed herself in the profitable exercise of " comparing spiritual things with spiritual ;" Scripture with itself; thus making God His own interpreter. Much light and heavenly unction she conceived herself to have gained by this means.'† The fruitfulness of this exercise will be, when we " find God's words" as our treasure ; " eat them" as our invigorating food ; and " they" thus become " the joy and rejoicing of our hearts." (Jer. xv. 16.) ' Set your affection'—saith the apocryphal writer— ' upon my words. Desire them, and ye shall be instructed. Wisdom is glorious, and never fadeth away ; yea, she is easily seen of those that love her, and found of such as seek her. She preventeth those that desire her, in making herself first known unto them. Whoso seeketh her early shall have no great travail ; for he shall find her sitting at his doors. Whoso watcheth for her ‡ shall quickly be without care. For she goeth about seeking such as are worthy of her, sheweth herself favourably unto them in the ways, and meeteth them, however, in every thought.'§

* *Life of Mary Jane Graham*, ut sup.

† Ib. Nicholls's Exposition of this Book, and Scott's Marginal References, will give much valuable assistance to this study. No foreign help, however, should damp the profitable interest of original research.

‡ 'Ο ἀγρυπνήσας — whom wisdom scarcely affords time to sleep.

§ Wisd. vi. 11-16. The reader will find throughout this Exposition frequent reference

An accurate apprehension of the main end and scope of this Book
will greatly facilitate the understanding of it.   Different portions of
Scripture may be seen to have different ends, all however subordinate
to one end — primary and supreme.   Without entering into detail
foreign to our purpose, suffice it to remark, that the end of this Book
appears to be, to set out a system of practical instruction, generally
applicable.   Nor let this be thought a low gradation in the Christian
scheme.   Unpalatable as it may be to the mere professor of godliness,°
the true man of God will honour practical inculcation in its place, no
less than doctrinal statement.   "The truth as it is in Jesus" — that
which flows from him, leads to him, and centres in him — that in which
"we are to be learned, and to be taught by him" — is practical truth.
(Eph. iv. 20–24.)   While other parts of Scripture shew us the glory of
our high calling ; this may instruct in all minuteness ,of detail how to
"walk worthy of it."   Elsewhere we learn our completeness in Christ
(Col. ii. 10) : and most justly we glory in our high exaltation as "joint-
heirs with Christ, made to sit together in heavenly places in Christ
Jesus." (Rom. viii. 17. Eph. ii. 6.)   We look into this Book, and, as by
the aid of the microscope, we see the minuteness of our Christian
obligations ; that there is not a temper, a look, a word, a movement,
the most important action of the day, the smallest relative duty, in
which we do not either deface or adorn the image of our Lord, and the
profession of his name.   Surely if the book conduced to no other end,
it tends to humble even the most consistent servant of God, in the
consciousness of countless failures.   Not only therefore is the last
chapter — as Matthew Henry would have it — 'a looking-glass for
ladies,' but the whole Book is a mirror for us all.

Nor is it only a mirror to shew our defects.   It is also a guide-

---

to the Apocryphal Books of Wisdom — *but only as human authorities*. Mr. Horne has most
demonstrably overthrown their claim to a place in the sacred canon. (*Introd. to Scrip.*
vol. i. Append. No. 1. last edit.) Yet while we would most distinctly mark the wide gulf
between inspired and uninspired writings, there seems no necessity to lose much valuable
and beautiful instruction, only because the writers were not inspired, or their writings were
tainted with pernicious errors.

° We fear that Mr. Scott's hearers at the Lock as a sect have not died away. Their real
objection — as his son admirably observed — 'was not to Arminianism (of which they
very probably scarcely knew the meaning) but to *half, or more than half the word of God.*
They had been accustomed to overlook it themselves, and could not bear to have it pressed
upon their notice by another.'— *Scott's Life,* pp. 232–235. Yet the preceptive part of an
Epistle may be set out, so dissociated from the doctrine, that the main-spring of practical
godliness is weakened, if not destroyed.

book and directory for godly conduct. The details of the external life, in all the diversified spheres, are given or implied with perfect accuracy, and with a profound knowledge of the workings of the human heart. ' Beside a code of laws directly religious, a variety of admirable rules stream forth from the deep recesses of wisdom, and spread over the whole field.'° All ranks and classes have their word in season. The sovereign on the throne is instructed as from God.[1] The principles of national prosperity or decay are laid open.[2] The rich are warned of their besetting temptations.[3] The poor are cheered in their worldly humiliation.[4] Wise rules are given for self-government.[5] ' It bridles the injurious tongue,[6] corrects the wanton eye,[7] and ties the unjust hand in chains.[8] It prevents sloth,[9] chastises all absurd desires;[10] teaches prudence;[11] raises man's courage;[12] and represents temperance and chastity after such a fashion, that we cannot but have them in veneration.'† To come to important matters so often mismanaged —the blessing or curse of the marriage ordinance is vividly pourtrayed.[13] Sound principles of family order and discipline are inculcated.[14] Domestic economy is displayed in its adorning consistency.[15] Nay—even the minute courtesies of daily life are regulated.[16] Self-denying consideration of others,[17] and liberal distribution[18] are enforced. All this diversified instruction is based upon the principles of true godliness.[19] Thus if the Psalms bring the glow upon the heart, the Proverbs "make the face to shine." Indeed the Writer may mention as one motive that led him to this work; that, having in a former Exposition‡ shewn at large Christian experience to be built upon the doctrines of the gospel, he wished to exhibit Christian practice as resting upon the same foundation. That is not sound faith, that does not issue in practical godliness. Nor is there any true morality, apart from

---

[1] Chap. viii. 15, 16; xvi. 10-13; xx. 8, 26; xxi. 1; xxv. 2-5; xxviii. 16; xxix. 14; xxxi. 1-9.
[2] Chap. xi. 14; xiv. 34; xxiv. 6; xxviii. 2. [3] Chap. xviii. 11; xxiii. 4, 5; xxviii. 20, 22.
[4] Chap. xv. 16, 17; xvii. 1; xix. 1, 22; xxviii. 6. [5] Chap. iv. 23-27; xvi. 32; xxiii. 1-3.
[6] Chap. iv. 24; x. 31; xvii. 20; xxv. 23; xxvi. 20-26.
[7] Chap. v. 20, 21; vi. 25-29; xxiii. 26, 27. [8] Chap. xviii. 5; xxviii. 8.
[9] Chap. vi. 6-11; xii. 27; xiii. 4; xix. 24; xx. 4; xxiv. 30-34. [10] Chap. xxi. 25, 26.
[11] Chap. iv. 14, 15; vi. 1-5; xiv. 8, 15, 18; xxii. 3; xxv. 6-10. [12] Chap. xxviii. 1.
[13] Chap. xviii. 22; xix. 14; xxxi. 10, with xii. 4; xix. 13; xxi. 9, 19.
[14] Chap. xiii. 24; xiv. 1; xix. 18; xxii. 6; xxiii. 13, 14; xxix. 15, 17, 19, 21.
[15] Chap. xxvii. 23-27; xxxi. 10-27. [16] Chap. xxiii. 6-8; xxv. 17. [17] Chap. iii. 27, 28.
[18] Chap. xi. 24; xxii. 9. [19] Chap. xxxi. 10, 30.
° Lord BACON's *Advancement of Learning*, Book viii. chap. ii.
† Chap. v. 15-19, with xxiii. 29-35. Basil, quoted by Bp. Patrick.
‡ On Ps. cxix.

"the principles of Christ." This Book, if it be not, as the New Testament,—the Rule of Faith, may surely be considered as a valuable Rule
of conduct. And—as Mr. Scott observes—'it would be very useful
for those, who can command their time, at some stated season every
day, to read and deliberately consider a few of these maxims, with
reference to their own conduct, in the various affairs in which they are
concerned.'⁰ Doubtless if the world were governed by the whole
wisdom of this single Book, it would be "a new earth, wherein
dwelleth righteousness."

One other weighty consideration the Writer would advert to, as
having directed his attention to this Book—*its distinctive character, as
a Book for the Young.* The wise man's father propounded a most
anxious question—"Wherewithal shall a young man cleanse his way?"
His son in this Book has fully opened the answer—"By taking heed
thereto according to thy word." (Ps. cxix. 9.) Nay he expressly states
the Book to be written for the heeding of youth.[1] It takes them as it
were by the hand, sets up way-marks to warn against coming danger
and imminent temptations,[2] and allures them into the bright ways of
God by the most engaging motives.[3] And never surely was the
object so momentous, as at the present day. Our young are growing
up at a period, when "the foundations of the earth are out of course;"
and when subtle and restless efforts are making to poison their hearts,
and pervert their ways. Nothing therefore can be more important, than
to fortify them with sound principles; that, when withdrawn from the
parental wing into a world or a Church (alas! that we should be constrained to use the term!) of temptation, they may be manifestly under
a Divine cover, as the children of a special Providence. What this
invaluable Book impresses upon their minds is, the importance of deep-
seated principles in the heart; the responsibility of conduct in every
step of life; the danger of trifling deviations for expediency's sake;
the value of self-discipline; the habit of bringing everything to the
Word of God; the duty of weighing in just balances a worldly and a
heavenly portion, and thus deciding the momentous choice of an everlasting good before the toys of earth. These lessons, thoroughly
inwrought, will prove the best security against all attempts to loosen

[1] Chap. i. 4; iv. 1, &c. [2] Chap. i. 10-15; ii. 10-19; v. 1-13; vii.
[3] Chap. iii. 1-18; viii. 17, &c.
⁰ Pref. to Comment. on Prov.

the hold of principle, and to entice upon enchanted ground. This practical godliness — so far from wearing a forbidding look, or being associated with gloom or sadness — casts a smile over a world of sorrow, is a sunbeam of comfort in suffering, and ever a principle of peace and steadfastness.   " Great peace have they which love thy law ; and nothing shall offend them." (Ps. cxix. 165.)

As to the matter of the exposition, the Writer cannot indeed say, with a Romish commentator,* 'that he has gone through all the circle of Biblical exposition, versions of the Scripture, Patristic reading, and classic literature bearing upon the Scripture.' He trusts, however, that it will be seen by the mass of references throughout the work, that he has taken due care to mature his own judgment, and to enlarge his scanty resources, by availing himself of the assistance of those expositors, who appear to have been most conversant with the original language, and to have given the most careful and sober interpretation. By a wider range, he would have probably rather perplexed than informed his readers.

He would not only add, in conclusion, in the words of one of the most valuable expositors † — that 'if there should be anything here to please the reader, ascribe not the writing to the pen, but to the writer ; not the light to the lamp, but to the fountain ; not the picture to the pencil, but to the painter ; not the gift to the unfaithful dispenser, but to God the bountiful Giver.'

* Cornelius à Lapide.   † Geier.

Old Newton Vicarage,
 Oct. 7, 1846.

ADVERTISEMENT

TO THE FOURTH EDITION.

THE Writer desires gratefully to acknowledge the many testimonies of interest and edification connected with his Work. Deeply sensible as he is of its great imperfections, may his God have the glory !

In reference to the mass of Scriptural references, he would state, that his primary object in this, as in a former Exposition, was to draw out into view the unsearchable riches of the Sacred field. And if he may have sometimes inadvertently carried out this desire to an undue extent, he trusts, that upon the whole it may encourage some of his Readers to a meditative study of Holy Writ, so that "the Word of Christ may dwell in them richly in all wisdom," to their own enlarged profit, and to the edification of the Church.

He has been enabled to compress the work (without abridgement), in order to reduce the price for wider circulation. He has now only to commend it afresh to the blessing of his God, and to the kind acceptance of His Church.

Hinton Martell Rectory,
July 16, 1859.

In accordance with suggestions repeatedly made to the Author the Exposition of the first nine chapters has been reprinted, apart, for more extensive distribution, under the title of " A MANUAL FOR THE YOUNG ;" *at the price of 2s. 6d.*

EXPOSITION OF THE BOOK OF PROVERBS.

CHAPTER I.

1. *The proverbs of Solomon, the Son of David, King of Israel ; 2. To know wisdom and instruction ; to perceive the words of understanding ; 3. To receive the instruction of wisdom, justice, and judgment, and equity ; 4. To give subtilty to the simple, to the young man knowledge and discretion.*

THE Book naturally opens with a short account of its author. Solomon is recorded as the wisest of men ; a man of wisdom, because a man of prayer. (1 Kings, iii. 12. Comp. chap. ii. 1–9.) His extraordinary wisdom was the admiration of the world. (1 Kings. iii. 28 ; iv. 34.) Had he been the son of Jeroboam, he would have commanded respect ; much more as *the son of David*, formed by his godly prayers (Ps. lxxii. 1) and counsels. (Chap. iv. 1–4. 1 Kings. ii. 1–4. 1 Chron. xxviii. 9.) And if a King's sayings, even though without intrinsic merit, are preserved ; the wise teaching of this *King of Israel* (Eccles. i. 1 ; xii. 9, 10) may well demand our especial interest.

Valuable, however, as were Solomon's maxims for their own wisdom (exceeding the sages of his own or any other time) (1 Kings, iv. 29–31) ; they claim our reverence upon infinitely higher ground. " Behold ! a greater than Solomon is here." (Matt. xii. 42.) Often does he speak in the person (Verse 20 ; viii. ix. xxiii. 26) always under the inspiration (2 Tim. iii. 16) of " the wisdom of God ;" so that his sayings are truly " *Divine* sentences in the lips of the King." (Chap. xvi. 10.)

The great end of this inestimable book is to teach, not secular or political wisdom (though many excellent rules of each are interspersed)

(Chap. vi. 1–11 ; xxvii. 23–27 ; with xi. 14 ; xiv. 28, 34 ; xx. 18) ; but that knowledge of God (Verse 7), which, while it "maketh wise unto salvation, perfects and furnishes the man of God unto all good works." (2 Tim. iii. 15–17. Tit. ii. 11, 12.) Its glowing privileges are set forth. (Chap. iii. 13–18.) It is pressed upon us with intense earnestness, as "the principal thing," our very "life." (Chap. iv. 5–9, 13.) *Instruction* is the means of gaining it. We are directed *to perceive the words of understanding ; to receive the instruction* as a complete rule *of wisdom, justice, judgment, and equity* (Comp. chap. ii. 9) ; sound principles, and their practical application. Here also *the simple,* so readily deluded (Chap. xiv. 15 ; xxi. 11. Ezek. xlv. 20), learn that *subtilty,* so needful to discriminate between truth and error (Philip. i. 10. 1 Thess. v. 21) ; to guard them from false teachers (Ps. xvii. 4. 1 John, iv. 1. Comp. Acts, xvii. 11) ; and to "convince gainsayers." (Tit. i. 9 ; ii. 8. Comp. Matt. xxii. 15–46.) Specially is *the young man* directed to this book.[*] His undisciplined ardour runs to waste. His mind fluctuates at the mercy of the winds of opinion in the world around him ; and greatly does he need some settled master-principles to fix his purpose, choice, and conduct. Here then he finds *knowledge and discretion ;* a religion, not of imagination, impulse, or sentiment ; but the sound practical energy of Scriptural truth.

> 5. *A wise man will hear, and will increase learning ; and a man of understanding shall attain unto wise counsels ; 6. To understand a proverb, and the interpretation ; the words of the wise, and their dark sayings.*

Not only *the simple and the young,* but even *the wise,* may here gather instruction. For a truly *wise man* is one, not who has attained, but who knows that he "has not attained," and is pressing onward to perfection. (Philip. iii. 12. Comp. 1 Cor. iii. 18 ; viii. 2.) David, while conscious of comparative attainments, was ever seeking for higher light. (Ps. cxix. 98–100 ; with 18, 33, 34.) Indeed the richest stores would soon waste, without constant additions. *Hearing* is a great medium of knowledge. Jethro instructed Moses (Exod. xviii. 17–26) ; our Lord his disciples. (Matt. xiii. 11–16. John, xvi. 12.) Peter enlightened his fellow-apostles. (Acts, xi. 2–18.) Priscilla and Aquila "instructed Apollos in the way of God more perfectly." (Ibid. xviii. 24–26.) Indeed we must be hearers, ere we would be teachers. 'He gathers that hears ; he spends that teacheth. If we spend before we gather, we shall soon prove bankrupts.'[†] The longer we learn, the more we feel ourselves to be learners ; and the more ready we shall be to *hear, that we*

---

[*] Ps. cxix. 9. Over the gates of Plato's school, it was written : Μηδιις αγιωμιτρητος ιισιτω. (Literally—Let no one who is not a geometrician enter.) But very different is the inscription over these doors of Solomon—Let the ignorant, simple, foolish, young enter. CARTWRIGHT *in loc.*—LAVATER in c. iv. 20–22.

[†] Bishop Hall.

may increase in learning. (Chap. ix. 9 ; xviii. 15.)   And at such a crisis
as this, both of the Church and of the world, how eagerly should we
improve every medium of instruction, by which we might become
" *men of understanding, and attain wise counsels,* to know what Israel
ought to do !" (1 Chron. xii. 32.)   The wise man himself expounded
his *words and dark sayings* to the delight and instruction of his royal
scholar (1 Kings, x. 1–5) ; so to a teachable *hearer* " the deep things
of God " will be *interpreted.* (1 Cor. ii. 9, 10.)   Hence the value of the
Minister of God ; " an interpreter, one of a thousand " (Job, xxxiii. 23.
Comp. Acts, viii. 27–35) ; the divinely-appointed mean of bringing to
the perfection of knowledge. (Eph. iv. 11–15. 1 Thess. iii. 10.)   Many
disorders and heresies might have been spared to the Church, if, instead
of indulging the perversity of an unsettled judgment, men had honoured
" the Priest, as the messenger of the Lord of Hosts," and in humble
simplicity had " sought the law at his mouth." (Mal. ii. 7. Comp. Heb.
xiii. 17, with 1 Cor. iv. 8 ; iii. 2–4.)   Self-will may resist this sugges-
tion as Romish domination.   But a humble subjection *to the faithful
" steward of the mysteries of God,"* coming to learn, not to teach ; to have,
not the curiosity fed, but the conscience satisfied.   This reverence of
God's ordinance will issue in the " good things of the heart established
with grace." (Heb. xiii. 9.)

7. *The fear of the Lord is the beginning* (principal part, marg.) *of know-
    ledge : but fools despise wisdom and instruction.*

The preface has stated the object of this Book of Wisdom.   The
book itself now opens with a noble sentence. ' There is not '— as Bishop
Patrick observes—' such a wise instruction to be found in all their
books (speaking of Heathen ethics), as the very first of all in Solomon's,
which he lays as the ground of all wisdom.' *   *The fear of the Lord is
the beginning of knowledge.*   So Job had pronounced before. (Job, xxviii.
28.)   So had the wise man's father. (Ps. cxi. 10.)   Such is the weight
of this saying, that Solomon again repeats it.†   Nay — after having
gone round the whole circuit ; after having weighed exactly all the
sources of knowledge ; his conclusion of the whole matter is this, that
the fear of God in its practical exercise " is the whole of man " (Eccles.
xii. 13.   Comp. Job, xxviii. 12–14, with 28)—all his duty ; all his
happiness ; his first lesson and his last.   Thus, when about to instruct
us from the mouth of God, he begins at *the beginning, the principal part.*
All heathen wisdom is but folly.   Of all knowledge, the knowledge of
God is the *principal.*   There is no true knowledge without godliness.
(Comp. Deut. iv. 6, 7.)

But what is this *fear of the Lord?*   It is that affectionate reverence,

* Preface to his Paraphrase.
† Chap. ix. 10   Comp. the fine description by the son of Sirach. Ecclus. i. 14-20, 27.

by which the child of God bends himself humbly and carefully to his Father's law. His wrath is so bitter, and his love so sweet ; that hence springs an earnest desire to please him, and—because of the danger of coming short from his own weakness and temptations—a holy watchfulness and *fear*, " that he might not sin against him." (Heb. xii. 28. 29.) This enters into every exercise of the mind, every object of life. (Chap. xxiii. 17.) The oldest proficient in the Divine school seeks a more complete moulding into its spirit. The godly parent trains up his family under its influence. (Gen. xviii. 19. Eph. vi. 4.) The Christian scholar honours it as *the beginning*, the head, *of all his knowledge;* at once sanctifying its end, and preserving him from its most subtle temptations.

Why then do multitudes around us *despise wisdom and instruction ?* Because *the beginning of wisdom*—" *the fear of God*—is not before their eyes." (Ps. xxxvi. 1.) They know not its value. They scorn its obligation. Wise they may be in their own sight. But surely God here gives them their right name. For *fools* they must be, to *despise* such a blessing (Jer. viii. 9) ; to rush into wilful ruin (Verses 22, 24–32. Comp. 1 Sam. ii. 25. 1 Kings, xii. 13. Jer. xxxvi. 22–32) ; to treasure up work for despairing repentance. (Chap. v. 12, 13 ; xxix. 1.) Good Lord ! May thy childlike *fear* be my *wisdom*, my security, my happiness !

8. *My son, hear the instruction of thy father, and forsake not the law of thy mother ; 9. For they shall be an ornament of grace unto thy head, and chains about thy neck.*

Let the young mark *the fear of the Lord* connected with reverence to parents. Thus the opening of this book puts honour upon " the first commandment with promise." (Eph. vi. 2. Comp. 1 Tim. v. 4.) God here, speaking by the mouth of a parent or teacher,[*] blends paternal tenderness with his Divine authority—*My son.* The command supposes the godly character of parents, and recognises the responsibility of *both* parents.[†] Children are rational creatures. *Instruction*, not blind submission, must be inculcated. Yet they are wayward. *Instruction* must therefore be enforced with the authority of *law.* God puts his own stamp upon parental discipline. *Hear it—Forsake it not.* Reverence for *his mother's law* was the honourable mark of Timothy's profession. (2 Tim. i. 5 ; iii. 14, 15.) Nor must this reverence be confined to the years of restraint. The disciple of the Bible will own himself to be a

---

* Thus the prophets were called Fathers—2 Kings, ii. 12; xiii. 14. Our blessed Lord used the same endearing address—John, xxi. 5. Comp. Matt. ix. 2, 22. Thus the Apostles also acknowledged both their individual converts and collective Churches—1 Tim. i. 2. 2 Tim. i. 2. Tit. i. 4. 1 Cor. iv. 15; with 1 John, ii. 1; v. 21.

† See Judg. xiii. 12. No ancient system, so fully as the Bible, recognises the Mother's just and equal claims. Comp. vi. 20 ; xv. 20; xx. 20; xxiii. 22; xxx. 17. Lev. xix. 3. Deut. xxi. 18–21. Cartwright observes, that the names of *Mothers* of good and bad kings are mentioned in Kings and Chronicles, as partakers in their credit or reproach. See also Ecclus. iii. 1–16.

child in relative obligations, long after he has ceased to be a child in years. (Jer. xxxv. 8–10, 18.) Neither age nor rank gives any claim for exemption. Joseph — when ripe in years, the head of a family, and the first Lord in Egypt — bowed before *his father's feet*. (Gen. xlvi. 29 ; xlviii. 12.) Solomon, in the glory of his crown, forgot not the respect justly due to *his mother*.[o] Nor were the crown *upon his head*, and *the chain* of gold *about Joseph's neck* (Comp. chap. iv. 9, with Gen. xli. 39, 42), so *graceful* as this *ornament* of filial humility. (1 Pet. v. 5.) This indeed commands the praise of the world, and may sometimes be a delusive, self-righteous dependence. But wherever it is grounded upon right principle, it is the "putting on of the Lord Jesus Christ" in his lovely example. (Rom. xiii. 14.) Though angels were subject to him, yet was he "subject to his parents." (Luke, ii. 51, with Heb. i. 6.) Yea, how did he honour his mother in his last dying command to his disciple — "Behold thy mother!" (John, xix. 27.)

The same reciprocal obligation binds, the spiritual father and his children. Authority softened by tenderness — *instruction* moulded in parental endearment — will always command its measure of reverential and affectionate attention. Such was the Apostolical Ministry to the Churches of Philippi and Thessalonica. Humility, tenderness, mutual communion and cheerful subjection, formed the harmony of Christian love and happiness. (Philip. iv. 9–19. 1 Thess. ii. 7–13.)

10. *My son, if sinners entice thee, consent thou not.* 11. *If they say, ' Come with us, let us lay wait for blood : let us lurk privily for the innocent without cause ; 12. Let us swallow them up alive as the grave ; and whole as those who go down into the pit ; 13. We shall find all precious substance ; we shall fill our houses with spoil : 14. Cast in thy lot among us ; let us all have one purse :' 15. My son, walk not thou in the way with them ; refrain thy foot from their path : 16. For their feet run to evil, and make haste to shed blood.*

Let the young *hearken to the instruction and law* of the godly parent and minister. Who that has the charge of youth does not mourn over the baneful influence of evil companions? Would that the Lord's servants were as energetic in his work, as *sinners* are in furthering the ends of their master! Almost as soon as Satan became an apostate, he became a tempter. And most successfully does he train his servants in this work. (Chap. xvi. 29. Gen. xi. 4. Num. xxxi. 16. Isa. lvi. 12.) *If sinners entice thee* — This is no uncertain contingency. 'My son' — said the wise son of Sirach — ' if thou come to serve the Lord prepare thy heart for temptation.' (Ecclus. ii. 1.) Yet we have one rule against all manifold enticements (Chap. vii. 5–23. Comp. Deut.

* 1 Kings, ii. 19, 20. See also Queen Esther's respect for Mordecai, her reputed father — ii. 20.

xiii. 6–8. 1 Chron. xxi. 1. 1 Kings, xiii. 15–19)— *Consent thou not. Consent* constitutes the sin. Eve *consented*, before she plucked the fruit (Gen. iii. 6) ; David, before he committed the act of sin. (2 Sam. xi. 2–4. Comp. Josh. vii. 21.) Joseph resisted, and was saved. (Gen. xxxix. 8, 9.) Job was sorely tried ; " yet in all this Job sinned not." (Job, i. 22 ; ii. 10.) If the temptation prevail, charge it not on God ; no—nor on the devil. As the worst he can do, he can only tempt, he cannot force us, to sin. When he has plied us with his utmost power, and most subtle artifice, it is at the choice of our own will, whether we yield or no. (See Jam. i. 13–15.) The habitual resistance of the will clears us of responsibility. (Comp. Rom. vii. 14–17, 19, 20, 23.) *The consent*, even if it be not carried out into the act, lays the responsibility at our own door.

The *enticement* here was to robbery and blood ; covetousness leading to murder. Most fiendish was the plot. *The innocent* was to be murdered *without cause* (Gen. iv. 8. Ps. x. 8), *swallowed up alive and whole ;* like Korah and his company, *going down into the pit* in their full strength. (Num. xvi. 33.) The invitation at first was seemingly harmless— Only *come with us.* Soon the demand rises— *Cast in thy lot with us!* ' But we shall be discovered.' No—they reply—' we will do all so cleverly, that there will be no more blood to be seen, than if the earth swallowed them up ; or they died a natural death, and were decently buried."[*] *The spoil of precious substance will be found,* when our victim is destroyed. (Comp. Matt. xxi. 38.) *Precious substance !* Why ! This is as large a promise, as that from the mouth of the Son of God. (Chap. viii. 21.) But how can *substance* be found belonging to a world of shadows ? (Ps. xxxix. 6.) Much more, how can the fruit of robbery be *precious*, with the curse of God ? (Chap. xxi. 6. Ps. lxii. 9, 10.)

Not that this horrible plot is usually propounded at first. But step by step, unless the Lord graciously restrains, it may come to this at last. The cover and varnish are here taken off, to show what sin is in its nature, character, and certain end. What young man, but would shudder, and start away from the wickedness, if presented to his imagination *alone ?* But many a deluded sinner is thus hurried on by the influence of company to lengths of sin, that he had never contemplated.[†] Other *enticements* are prepared for the amiable and the uninitiated, just entering into life ; less fearful and obvious, and therefore more really dangerous. Such " advantage does Satan get of us by our ignorance of his devices !" (2 Cor. ii. 11.)

Is it safe then to trust in our good resolutions or principles ? No — *Walk not in the way with them.* The invitation is— *Come with us.* The warning is— *Refrain thy foot from their path.* (Chap. iv. 14, 15.

---

[*] Cartwright   But see Gen iv. 10. 2 Kings. ix. 26.
[†] Chartist Associations afford ample evidence of this awful delusion.

Comp. Ps. i. 1.) Avoid parleying with them. No one becomes a pro-fligate at once.* But "evil communications corrupt good manners." (1 Cor. xv. 33.) The tender conscience becomes less sensitive by every compliance. Who can stop himself in the down-hill road? One sin prepares for another, pleads for it, nay, even makes it necessary for con-cealment. David committed murder to hide his adultery, and for his covering charged it upon the providence of God. (2 Sam. xi. 4, 17, 25.)

Again then — we repeat with all earnestness — *Refrain. The path* may be strewed with flowers; but it is a path of *evil,* perhaps of *blood.*† Every step on Satan's ground deprives us of the security of the promises of God. Often has ruin followed by not *refraining* from the first step. (Comp. Mark, xiv. 54, 71.) The only safety is in flight. (Gen. xxxix. 10, 12.) Run then into "thy hiding-place, and behind thy shield," and boldly bid thy tempter "depart from thee." (Ps. cxix. 114, 115. Comp. Matt. iv. 10.) Awful is the thought! There is not a sin, that the highest saint of God may not commit, if trusting in himself. "Thou standest by faith. Be not high-minded, but fear." (Rom. xi. 20.)

17. (*Surely in vain the net is spread in the sight of any bird.*) 18. *And they lay wait for their own blood; they lurk privily for their own lives.* 19. *So are the ways of every one that is greedy of gain; which taketh away the life of the owners thereof.*

The sight of danger leads, when possible, to the avoiding of it. Instinct directs the bird; reason the man. Yet such is the infatuation of sin, that man in his boasted wisdom will not do, what the bird will do by her native instinct. She shuns *the net spread in her sight;* man rushes into it. These men thirsted for their neighbour's *blood.* But in the end *they laid wait for their own.* They *lurked privily* for the innocent *without cause.* But it proved to be *lurking privily for their own lives.* (Verse 11 with 18. Comp. Job, xviii. 8. Hab. ii. 10.) Ahab and his guilty partner, in plotting the destruction of their *innocent* victim, worked out their own ruin. (1 Kings, xxi. 4–24.) Little did Haman, when bent upon the murder of Mordecai (Esth. vii. 9); or Judas, when "seek-ing opportunity to betray his Master" (Matt. xxvi. 14–16; xxvii. 3–5), see, that they were "digging a pit for themselves." (Ps. vii. 15, 16; ix. 15, 16.) Yet the sinner, would he but use his own eyes, might see hell at the end of his path. (Matt. vii. 13.) But sin is self-delusive, self-destructive. So are the ways — such the end — of *greedy,* often mur-derous, *gain.*‡ *My son* — once more *hear thy Father's instruction,* "Flee these things." (Verse 8, with 1 Tim. vi. 9–11.)

---

* 'Nemo fit repente turpissimus.'—Classical adage.
† Verse 16. Isa. lix. 7. An apt illustration of the total depravity of man in the perverted use of the members of his body.—Rom. iii. 15.
‡ Comp. Job, xxxi. 39, 40. Jer. xxii. 17-19. Mic. iii. 10-12. 'How great a cheat is wickedness! It ensnareth the ensnarers, and murders the murderers; holds a dark lantern in one hand, while with the other it discharges silently a pistol into our bosom.'—JERMIN (Dr. M.), *Comment on Proverbs,* folio, 1638.

20. *Wisdom* (Wisdoms, Marg.) *crieth without; she uttereth her voice in the streets :* 21. *She crieth in the chief place of concourse, in the openings of the gates ; in the city she uttereth her words, saying,* 22. *How long, ye simple ones, will ye love simplicity? and the scorners delight in their scorning, and fools hate knowledge?* 23. *Turn you at my reproof: behold, I will pour out my Spirit unto you; I will make known my words unto you.*

A Father's instruction has warned us against the enticement of Satan. *Wisdom* — the Son of God himself, now invites us,— in all the plenitude of his Divine authority and grace.° Full of yearning love to sinners, he *crieth,* not only in the temple, but *without in the streets, in the chief place of concourse, in the openings of the gates* (Comp. chap. viii. 1–5. Matt. xiii. 2. John, vii. 37–39 ; xviii. 20, 21. Ps. xl. 9, 10)—*How long? Simplicity* is another term for folly. It is the temper of mind of those that fear not God. They weigh not what they say or do. They live as if there were neither God nor eternity. Their understandings are blinded by the love of sin. In other cases man delights, not in his ignorance, but in its removal. But these *simple ones,* ignorant of the value and danger of their souls, *love simplicity.* They consider all endeavours to enlighten them, as breaking in upon an indulgent repose, and exciting a groundless alarm. For while they live riotously, slothfully, or licentiously, "they consider not in their hearts, that God remembereth all their wickedness," and " that for all these things he will bring them into judgment." (Hos. vii. 2. Eccles. xi. 9.) They are encouraged by a few more furious than themselves—*scorners*—who have neither fear nor shame, remorse of heart, nor decency of manner ; who take an active *delight in their scorning :* shooting their poisoned arrows against godliness. (See Ps. lxiv. 3, 4.) All earnestness in religion is with them a weakness unworthy of sensible men. The very Scripture terms are revolting. A saint in Scripture means one sanctified by the Spirit of God. With them it means a foolish person or a hypocrite. Their souls are too high to stoop to the vulgar thoughts and habits of the gospel of Christ. Thus do they prove themselves (both the indolent mass of the *simple ones,* and their *scornful* leaders) to be *fools, that hate knowledge.*

* *The cry, the chief place of concourse, the outpouring fountain of the Spirit,* are identified John, vii. 37–39. This very remonstrance, accompanied, as here, with a stirring invitation, is also given in prophecy from the Saviour's own mouth. Isa. lv. 1–3. The terms of the promise forbid any other than a personal application. We can easily conceive a spirit to have wisdom. But that an attribute of wisdom may dispense his Spirit or influence to others, is beyond conception. Moreover, the Messiah assumed this personal title (Matt. xxiii. 34, with Luke, xi. 49); and his Apostle expressly gives it to him (1 Cor. i. 24). The plural noun joined with the singular verb (marg. comp. chap. ix. 1) seems to point him out as the author and whole substance of all wisdom ; 'the very wisdom of the most wise God, " in whom are hid all the treasures of wisdom and knowledge," and by whom rivers of wisdom are poured into man by the word.' (Glass. Lib. iii. Tract. i. Can. 24.) The future tense in the original may possibly give a prophetic character to the proclamation. Altogether, 'this interpretation gives to the exhortation of Wisdom a peculiar majesty and emphasis ; setting forth the eternal uncreated Wisdom of the Father, using all means to draw men to God : both by his works and by his word, inviting all men to know the truth.'—Scott. Bishop Hall. Compare notes on v. 24. viii. 1.

(Verses 7, 29, 30. Job, xxi. 14 ; xxiv. 13.) Aiming to keep out alarm, with it they shut out all that would make them wise and happy. If they *hate the knowledge* of their lost condition, they exclude all that follows upon it, to make them " wise unto salvation." Of other knowledge they have often too much : mischievous, as keeping out better things ; giving them an evil eye, filling the soul with darkness ; making them " hate the light, so that they will not come to the light, lest their deeds should be reproved." (John, iii. 19, 20.)

Our Lord deals with this case on the perfect freeness of the gospel. He would melt down the hardness by pleading remonstrance — *How long ?* (Comp. Matt. xxiii. 37. Luke, xix. 41, 42.) He sweeps away all the suggestions of unbelief, all the heartless excuses of indolence, by inviting promises — *Turn at my reproof.* ' I cannot turn myself.' But *I will pour out my Spirit* as a living fountain *unto you.* And — as the consequence of this blessing — *I will make known my words unto you.* The Bible, before a dark and sealed book, shall be made clear to you. ' I offer to you both my word outwardly to your ears, and a plentiful measure of my Spirit inwardly to your heart, to make that word effectual to you.' °

But we are often told, that all the illumination to be expected in our day is the written word, interpreted, like every other book, by our own reason ; and that the Spirit's teaching is an enthusiastic delusion. Now this may pass with the *simple and the scorner* — who know nothing of the blindness of their hearts, and of the power of natural prejudice, which Divine grace alone can conquer. But the man that knows his own darkness, and that nothing less than the power of God can teach him — he will — he must — " cry for knowledge, and lift up his voice for understanding " (Chap. ii. 3) ; not because the word is dark (for it is light itself), but because he is dark, and therefore utterly unable to receive its instructions. (1 Cor. ii. 9–14.) We do not want a new revelation, we only want a Divine Teacher, we want *the pouring out of the Spirit to make known the word.* The word is the same Divine word as before. But it was not understood, discerned, not therefore practically effectual. *Now* there is joy, a power and sweetness, of which before we had no conception. It humbled us in the sense of our ignorance, and makes us pant for more of its heavenly light and influence.

But the proud caviller complains of God, as if he reckoned with him for a blindness and inability, which he cannot help,— innate without his consent. " Nay, but, O man, who art thou that. repliest against God ?" (Rom. ix. 20.) He at once answers this Satanic plea, by offering to you present, suitable, and sufficient relief. He meets you on your way to condemnation with the promise of free and full

* Bishop Hall.

forgiveness. (Isa. i. 18 ; xliii. 23, 26.)   Your plea will be of force, when
you have gone to him, and found him wanting.   The power indeed is
of him.   But he hath said — " Ask, and it shall be given you." (Matt.
vii. 7.)   If your helplessness is a real grievance, bring it to him with
an honest desire to be rid of it.   If you have never prayed, now is the
time for prayer.   If you cannot pray, at least make the effort.   Stretch
out the withered hand in the obedience of faith. (Mark, iii. 5.)   If your
heart be hard, your convictions faint, your resolutions unsteady ; all is
provided in the promise — *I will pour out my Spirit upon you.*   Move
then, and act in dependence upon the Almighty Mover and Agent.
(Comp. Philip. ii. 12, 13.)   Christian experience explains a mystery unfathomable to human reason.   It harmonises man's energy and God's
grace.   There is no straitening, no exclusion, with God.   His promises
with one mouth assure a welcome to the willing heart.   If it cannot
move, his Spirit can compel, point, draw it to the Saviour.   Yea, in the
desire to turn, has not the Saviour already touched it, and drawn it to
himself ?

But remember — the call — *How long ?* is to an instant conversion ;
not to the consideration or resolution of the morrow, but to the decision of to-day.   Delay is mockery of God.   " Quench not the
Spirit " now striving, but which " will not always strive with man."
(1 Thess. v. 19.   Gen. vi. 3.)   Add not thus to the mass of guilt ready
to sink you into perdition.

24. *Because I have called, and ye refused ; I have stretched out my hand,*
    and no man regarded : 25. But ye have set at nought all my counsel,
    and would none of my reproof : 26. I also will laugh at your calamity ;
    I will mock, when your fear cometh ; 27. When your fear cometh as a
    desolation, and your destruction cometh as a whirlwind ; when distress
    and anguish cometh upon you.   28. Then shall they call upon me, but
    I will not answer ; they shall seek me early, but they shall not find me ;
    29. For that they hated knowledge, and did not choose the fear of the
    Lord : 30. They would none of my counsel : they despised all my reproof.
    31. Therefore shall they eat of the fruit of their own way, and be filled
    with their own devices.

The Saviour *calls* by his word, his providence, his ministers, conscience.   But *ye refused.*   Not till his *calls* have been *refused*, does he
thunder forth his warnings.   But such grace, so rich and free, yet
rejected — who can take the guage of this guilt ?   All creatures beside
are his servants. (Ps. cxix. 91.)   Man alone resists his yoke.   *He*
stretched out his hand (Isa. lxv. 2) to afford help ; to confer a blessing ;
to beseech its acceptance ; yea, even to command attention to his call.
(See Acts, xxi. 40.)   But *no man regarded.*   The wisest *counsel*, the most
solemn *reproof,* all is *set at nought.*   Thus does he " endure with much

long-suffering the vessels of wrath fitted to destruction." (Rom. ix. 22.) But, O sinner! the day cometh, when he, who once yearned, and wept, and prayed, and died, will have no pity (Ezek. v. 11. viii. 18, with xxxiii. 11) ; when he shall be, as if he *laughed and mocked at your calamity* (Comp. Judg. x. 14. Isa. i. 24); when he shall delight in the exercise of his sovereign justice over you. (Comp. Deut. xxviii. 63. Ezek. v. 13.) All will then be the *desolation* of realized *fear* (Chap. x. 24); sudden *as a whirlwind;** the *distress and anguish* of utter despair. (Job, xv. 24. Dan. v. 5, 6, 30.)

This is his solemn denunciation. And then, as if he could bear these despisers no longer in his sight, he changes his address, and pictures the scene itself in its strongest colours. *They* would not hear when I called. *Then shall they call upon me, and I will not answer.* They would not listen to my warnings ; I will not listen to their cries. *They shall call upon me* — yea, *they shall seek me early; but they shall not find me.*† Prayer, once omnipotent, will then be powerless. 'The last judgment before the very last of all is come ; the very outward court or portal of hell ;'‡ the misery of deserted souls. To be forsaken of God at any time is awful woe (Hos. ix. 12) ; how much more in the time of trouble! (1 Sam. xxviii. 15.) But to have his countenance not only turned from us, but turned against us, his eternal frown instead of his smile — this will be hell instead of heaven.

Does this unmeasured wrath seem inconsistent with a God of love? "The Lord our God is a consuming fire." (Deut. iv. 24.) And think of his *knowledge*, instead of being a delight, being *hated; his fear not chosen;* none of his gracious *counsel* regarded ; all his *reproof despised.* Is it not just, that the sinner, thus obstinately bent upon the choice of *his own way*, should not only gather, but *eat the fruit of it?* (Chap. xiii. 2) ; that it should enter into him, and become his substance ; that he should be *filled with it*, even to satiety ;§ *and that* — not only during his road (Num. xi. 4, 20. Ps. cvi. 13–15), but at the end, throughout eternity? (Isa. iii. 11. Gal. vi. 7.) The moral elements of sin constitute a hell of themselves, apart from the material fire. 'The fruit of sin in time, when arrived at full and finished maturity, is just the fruit of sin

* Chap. x. 25. Ps. lviii. 9. Isa. xvii. 13 ; xl. 24. Eastern travellers furnish abundant illustration of this striking figure. Paxton's *Illustrations of Scripture Geography*, pp. 412-416. — (Oliphant.)

† Matt. xxv. 6-12. Luke, xiii. 24-26. Dr. Owen admirably remarks upon this remonstrance as a proof of the Personality of Wisdom — ' If these things express not a person, and *that* a Divine person, the Scripture gives us no due apprehension of anything whatever. Who is it that pours out the Holy Spirit? Who is it that men sin against, in refusing to be obedient? Who is it, that in their distress they call upon, and seek early in their trouble? The whole Scriptures declare to whom, and to whom alone, these things belong, and may be ascribed.' -- *Expos. of Hebrews.* Prelim. Exercit. xxvii 8-12. We might add — Who besides could threaten rebels with ruin, and promise peace and security to the obedient?

‡ Bishop Reynolds' Works, p. 971.

§ Chap. xiv. 14. Comp. xxv. 16. — ' Ad nauseam implebuntur, et comedent, ita ut consiliorum vehementer tandem, sed nimis sero, ipsos pœnitcant.'--MICHAELIS.

through eternity. It is merely the sinner reaping what he has sown. It makes no violent or desultory step from sin in time to hell in eternity. The one emerges from the other, as does the fruit from the flower. It is simply, that the sinner *be filled with his own ways, and that he eat the fruit of his own devices.'*

This picture might seem to be the foreboding of despair. Yet, such miracles of Divine grace have we seen ; nay — such are we ourselves — that we despair of none. We must not, however, soften down God's own words by a misplaced presumptuous tenderness. Have we never seen them verified in the dying sinner, who has neglected and scoffed at the Gospel, and never sent up one cry for mercy on his soul ? Is this no warning of the danger of *a protracted* repentance ; of the worthlessness of confessions extorted by terror ; " howling on the bed, not weeping at the cross ? " (Hos. vii. 14, with Luke, xviii. 13.) And does it not solemnly tell us, that the day of grace has its limits (Gen. vi. 3. Heb. iv. 7) ; that there is a knock, which will be the last knock ; that a sinner may be lost on this side of hell ; intreated, pleaded with, wept over — yet lost ! lost even in the day of salvation ? To " do despite to the Spirit *of grace* " (mark the endearing name) — the Spirit of all kindness, of alluring love ; who pleads so tenderly with us — to wound him, as it were, to the soul (Heb. x. 29, Gr.) — this is a provocation beyond words, beyond thought. " There remaineth " only that, which might strike into the very centre of the man, " the fearful looking for of judgment and fiery indignation, which shall devour the adversaries. It is a fearful thing to fall into the hands of the living God." (Ib. verses 26, 27, 31.)

32. *For the turning away of the simple shall slay them, and the prosperity of fools shall destroy them.* **33.** *But whoso hearkeneth unto me shall dwell safely, and shall be quiet from fear of evil.*

Again is the sinner's ruin laid at his own door. He *turns away* from Wisdom's beseeching voice. He despises the only remedy. He dies a suicide. It matters nothing to what we turn. If we *turn away* from God, we turn from our true, our eternal interests. And, oh ! be it remembered, that every inattention, every wilful neglect, is a step towards this fearful apostasy. The word gradually becomes a burden, then a scorn. *The fool* may seem to be spared from judgment. But *his prosperity is his destruction.*† To desire ease, therefore, is to embrace a deadly enemy. Who that knows his own heart will not feel it a matter, not of congratulation, but of deep and anxious prayer — ' In all time of our wealth — Good Lord, deliver us ? '‡

---

* Chalmers on Rom. vi. 21.
† Job, xxi. 11-13. Ps. lv. 19 ; lxxiii. 3-20. Jer. xii. 1-3. Luke, vi. 24, 25 ; xii. 16-20 ; xvi. 19-24. Jam. v. 1-5. Examples of Israel. — Deut. xxxii. 15-25. Jer. xxii. 20-22. Hos xiii. 6-9. Amos, vi. 1-6. Babylon.— Isa. xlvii. 7-9. Moab.— Jer. xlviii. 11-15. Sodom. —Ezek. xvi. 49. Tyre.—Ezek. xxvii. 2, 25-27.   ‡ Litany.

But to close with the sunshine of promise — Art thou, Reader, like God's own child, *hearkening unto him?* Then art thou under his cover, where no evil can reach thee ; *dwelling* not only *safely*, but assured of safety ; *quiet even from fear of evil* (Chap. iii. 21–26. Job, v. 21. Ps. xci. 5; cxii. 6, 7. Isa. xxxii. 17–19); as Noah in the ark, in conscious security, while the world were perishing around him (Gen. vii. 11–16); as David, fearless in imminent danger, because realizing a refuge in God. (Ps. iii. Comp. 1 Sam. xxx. 6.) Yes — even the *coming day of distress and anguish* brings with it no *fear of evil.* (Contrasting verses 26, 27. Luke, xxi. 26. Rev. vi. 16–18.) "The day will burn like an oven." Thou shalt behold the world on fire, and feel thou hast lost, thou canst lose, nothing. The "day of darkness and gloominess" will be to thee a day of unclouded sunshine, the entrance into everlasting joy. (Mal. iv. 1, 2. Luke, xxi. 28. 2 Pet. iii. 10–13.)

CHAPTER II.

1. *My son, if thou wilt receive my words, and hide my commandments with thee; 2. So that thou incline thine ear unto wisdom, and apply thine heart to understanding : 3. Yea, if thou criest after knowledge, and liftest up thy voice for understanding ; 4. If thou seekest her as silver, and searchest for her as for hid treasures ; 5. Then shalt thou understand the fear of the Lord, and find the knowledge of God. 6. For the Lord giveth wisdom: out of his mouth cometh knowledge and understanding.*

Wisdom, having solemnly warned rebellious scorners, now instructs her dutiful children. The dark question long before asked —"Where shall wisdom be found?" (Job, xxviii. 12, 20, 21) — is now answered. It is here set before us, as *the fear and knowledge of God* (Verse 5) ; a principle of practical godliness (Verses 7–9) ; a preservation from besetting temptations (Verses 10–19) ; and a guide into the right and safe path. (Verse 20.) Hence follow the security of its scholars (Verse 21), and the certain ruin of its ungodly despisers. (Verse 22.)

The rules for its attainment are such as the simplest comprehension can apply. Carefully pondered, and diligently improved, they will furnish a key for the understanding of the whole word of God. Let us examine them more distinctly.

Receive my words — Let them be "the seed cast into the ground of an honest and good heart" (Luke, viii. 15) — a heart prepared of God. (Chap. xvi. 1.) Read the book of God as one who "sat at the feet of Jesus, and heard his word." (Luke, x. 39.) Like the Bereans, "receive it with all readiness" (Acts, xvii. 11); like the Thessalonians, with reverential faith, acknowledging its supreme authority (1 Thess. ii. 13).

Hide my commandments with thee. Carry them about with thee as thy choicest treasure for greater security (Col. iii. 16, with Matt. xiii. 44) ; as thy furniture always at hand for present use. (Chap. iv. 20, 21 ; vii. 3. Job, xxii. 22.) Let the heart be the hiding-place for the treasure. (Luke, ii. 19, 51. Ps. cxix. 11.) Satan can never snatch it thence.

But there must be an active, practical habit of attention.[*] Yet to *incline the ear, and apply the heart*—" who is sufficient for these things ? " Oh ! my God ! let it be thine own work on me — in me. Thou alone canst do it.[†] Let it be with me, as with thy Beloved Son —" Waken my ear morning by morning to hear as the learned." (Isa. L. 4.) So let me under thy grace " incline mine ear, and hear, that my soul may live." (Ibid. lv. 3.)

Without this spirit of prayer—there may be attention and earnestness ; yet not one spiritual impression upon the conscience ; not one ray of Divine light in the soul. Earthly wisdom is gained by study ; heavenly wisdom by prayer. Study may form a Biblical scholar ; prayer puts the heart under a heavenly tutorage, and therefore forms the wise and spiritual Christian. The word first comes into the ears ; then it enters into the heart ; there it is safely hid ; thence rises *the cry* — *the lifting up of the voice.* Thus, " the entrance of thy word giveth light ; it giveth understanding to the simple." (Ps. cxix. 130.) God keeps the key of the treasure-house in his own hand. " For this he will be enquired of" (Ezek. xxxvi. 37) to open it unto thee. We look for no other inspiration than Divine grace to make his word clear and impressive. Every verse read and meditated on furnishes material for prayer. Every text prayed over opens a mine of " unsearchable riches," with a light from above, more clear and full than the most intelligent exposition. David (Ps. cxix. 18, &c.) and his wise son (1 Kings, iii. 9–12) sought this learning upon their knees ; and the most matured Christian will continue to the end to *lift up his voice* for a more enlarged *knowledge of God.* (Eph. i. 17, 18.)

But prayer must not stand in the stead of diligence. Let it rather give energy to it.[‡] The miner's indefatigable pains ; his invincible

---

[*] Chap. xxii. 17 ; xxiii. 12. The Emperor Constantine stood hours to hear the word ; replying, when asked to sit, 'that he thought it wicked to give negligent ears, when the truth handled was spoken of God.'—(*Euseb. de Vita Constant.* lib. iv.) Foxe records of Edward VI. 'That never was he present at any sermon commonly, but would excerp them, or note them with his own hand.'—Vol. v. 700. Yet Bishop Hooper thought, that his royal master's love for the preached word needed to be quickened. — *Sermon 7th on Jonas.*

[†] Chap. xx. 12. "Thou giving me the ear, I have heard, as thou wouldest thy word to be heard."—JEROME *on Hab.* iii. 2.

[‡] On one side is Luther's inestimable axiom — ' Bene orasse est bene studuisse.' On the other side is the balance of the old proverb—' Ora et labora.' Comp. Matt. xi. 12. We are all,' says the heavenly Leighton, ' too little in the humble seeking and begging this Divine knowledge ; and that is the cause why we are so shallow and small proficients. " If thou cry, and lift up thy voice for understanding, search for it as for hid treasures ;" sit down upon thy knees, and dig for it. That is the best posture, to fall right upon the golden vein, and go deepest to know the mind of God, in searching the Scriptures, to be

resolution; his untiring perseverance; *seeking, yea, searching for hid treasures,*— such must be our *searching* into the sacred storehouse.* To read, instead of "*searching* the Scriptures," is only to skim the surface, and gather up a few superficial notions.† The rule of success is — Dig up and down the field; and if the search be discouraging, dig again. The patient industry of perusal and re-perusal will open the embosomed treasure. "Surely there is a vein for the silver." (Job, xxviii. 1.) Yet what miner would be content with the first ore? Would he not *search* deeper and deeper, until he has possessed himself of the whole; not satisfied with taking away much, but determined to leave nothing? Thus let us daily explore "the length, and the breadth, and the depth" of our boundless stores, until we be "filled with all the fulness of God." (Eph. iii. 18, 19.)

This habit of living in the element of Scripture is invaluable. To be filled from this Divine treasury; to have large portions of the word daily passing through the mind; gives us a firmer grasp, and a more suitable and diversified application of it. Yet this profit can only be fully reaped in retirement. We may read the Scriptures in company. But to *search* them, we must be alone with God. Here we learn to apply ourselves wholly to the word, and the word wholly to us. This enriching study gives a purer vein of sound judgment. The mere reader often scarcely knows where to begin, and he performs the routine without any definite object. His knowledge therefore must be scanty and ineffective. Nor is the neglect of this habit less hurtful to the Church. All fundamental errors and heresies in the Church may be traced to this source—"Ye do err, not knowing the Scriptures." (Matt. xxii. 29.) They are mostly based on partial or disjointed statements of truth. Truth separated from truth becomes error. But the mind prayerfully occupied in the *search* of Divine truth—*crying and lifting up the voice*— will never fail to discern the two great principles of godli-

directed and regulated in his ways; to be made skilful in ways of honouring him, and doing him service. This neither man nor angels can teach him, but God alone.'—*Sermon on Ps.* cvii. 43.

* 'Viscera terræ extrahimus, ut digito gestiatur gemma, quam petimus. Quot manus afferuntur, ut unus niteat articulus! Simili studio, industriâ, constantiâ, Sapientiæ inquisitioni incumbendum erat.'—PLIN. lib. ii. c. 65.

† Comp. John, v. 39. Gr.—a similar allusion to the miner's toil. 'I can speak it by experience'— said a wise man—'that there is little good to be gotten by reading the Bible cursorily and carelessly. But do it daily and diligently, with attention and affection; and you shall find such efficacy, as is to be found in no other book that can be named.'— ERASMUS's *Preface to Luke.* Peter Martyr gives the same testimony, *Epist. Dedic. to Comment. on Rom.* The following relic of our renowned Elizabeth will be read both with interest and profit. It was written on a blank leaf of a black-letter edition of St. Paul's Epistles, which she used during her lonely imprisonment at Woodstock. The volume itself, curiously embroidered by her own hand, is preserved in the Bodleian :—'August. I walk many times into the pleasant fields of the Holy Scriptures, where I pluck up the goodlisome herbs of sentences by pruning, eat them by reading, chew them by musing, and lay them up at length in the high seat of memorie, by gathering them together, that so, having tasted their sweetness, I may the less perceive the bitterness of this miserable life.'—MISS STRICKLAND's *Queens of England*, vi. 113.

ness — *The fear and knowledge of God.* There is no peradventure nor disappointment in this search — *Then shalt thou understand. The Lord giveth wisdom; it cometh out of his mouth.* None shall search in vain. (Job, xxxii. 8. Isa. xlviii. 17 ; liv. 13. Jam. i. 5, 17. Comp. Gen. xli. 38, 39. Exod. iv. 12. Dan. i. 17.) Never has apostasy from the faith been connected with a prayerful and diligent study of the word of God.

7. *He layeth up sound wisdom for the righteous : he is a buckler to them that walk uprightly.* 8. *He keepeth the paths of judgment, and preserveth the way of his saints.* 9. *Then shalt thou understand righteousness, and judgment, and equity ; yea every good path.*

Vanity (Eccles. i. 18) and foolishness (1 Cor. iii. 19) are the stamp on the wisdom of this world. Here is *sound wisdom.* It looks at things not in their notions, but in their proper substance. It is *sound,* because it is practical. It is indeed a *hid treasure* (Verse 4) ; so safe, that no spoiler can reach it ; yet so free, that every sinner may have access to it. Yes ; in the Son of God himself " are hid all the treasures of wisdom and knowledge." All these treasures in him are *laid up for the righteous* —made over to them. (Col. ii. 3. 1 Cor. i. 30.) Oh let us draw upon this infinite treasure daily, hourly, for light to direct *an upright walk.* 'To those that are true and *upright* in heart, he will in his own good time reveal true and saving knowledge, and that *sound* spiritual *wisdom,* which shall make them eternally happy.'° Our faithful God *is a buckler to them that walk uprightly.* (Chap. xxx. 5. Ps. lxxxiv. 11.) His wisdom covers us from that subtle sophistry, which would spoil us of our treasure. (Chap. xxii. 12.) The way of the saints is indeed fraught with danger ; beset with temptation : yet is it safe (Chap. iv. 11 ; viii. 20. Deut. xxxiii. 26–29. 1 Sam. ii. 9. Ps. xxxvii. 23, 24 ; lvi. 9) — *kept and preserved by* Almighty power, even on the very edge of the enemy's ground. (1 Sam. xxv. 39 ; xxvii. 1, with xxix. 2 Cor. xii. 7–9.)

Such also is the completeness of this godly privilege, that not only does it enlarge our *knowledge of God* (Verse 5), but it brings us to a full *understanding* of every practical obligation. Indeed that only is *sound wisdom,* that guides our feet into *every good path;* that " makes the man of God perfect, throughly furnished unto all good works." (2 Tim. iii. 15–17.) The gracious *wisdom* that saves the soul, sanctifies the heart and life. (Tit. ii. 11, 12.)

10. *When wisdom entereth into thine heart, and knowledge is pleasant unto thy soul;* 11. *Discretion shall preserve thee, understanding shall keep thee.*

We have seen the good that *wisdom* brings to us. (Verse 5.) Now see the evil, from which it *preserves* us. But observe its place — *in the*

° Bishop Hall.

heart. Here only has it any light, life, or power. (Chap. iv. 23.) Clear knowledge floating in the head is deep ignorance. While it only glitters in the understanding, it is dry, speculative, and barren. *When it entereth into the heart,* light beams out, all the affections are engaged ; and how *pleasant is it to the soul!* (Chap. xxiv. 13, 14. Job, xxiii. 12. Ps. cxix. 103. Jer. xv. 16.) Religion *now* is no lifeless notion. It is handled, tasted, enjoyed. It gives a *discreet and understanding* direction to the whole conduct. It becomes not only an external rule, but a *preserving, keeping* principle (Chap. iv. 6 ; vi. 22–24. Ps. xvii. 4 ; cxix. 9–11, 104) ; like the military guard for the safety of the royal person. (1 Sam. xxvi. 16. 2 Kings, xi. 11.) Before, it was the object of our search. Now, having found it, it is our *pleasure.* Until it is so, it can have no practical influence. It is " the man, whose *delight is in the law of the Lord,*" who is preserved from " walking in the counsel of the ungodly." (Ps. i. 1, 2 ; comp. ch. vii. 4, 5.) Education, conviction, high moral principle, are at best only partially operative. The reclaimed drunkard may be true to his Temperance-pledge ; but, if the " root of bitterness " be untouched, he may be a Socialist or a Chartist, or revel in some other equally ruinous course. External wickedness may be exchanged for decent formality. Vagrant affections may be turned from some object of vanity ; yet not fixed upon the Divine centre of attraction. The mind may be disciplined from utter unprofitableness, only to indulge in the idolatry of talent, or the fascinations of poisoned literature. The folly of the pride of life may be resisted ; yet pride in other of its multiform fruits tenderly cherished. In all these cases, the principle is unsubdued. The forsaken sin only makes way for some more plausible, but not less deadly passion. The heart, cast into the mould of the Gospel, is the only cover from those snares within and without (Rom. vi. 17, 18. 2 Cor. iii. 18); which so imperceptibly, yet so fatally, estrange us from God. Never, till the vital principle is implanted, is their mischief discerned. Never, till then, does the heart find its proper object, its true resting-place.

12. *To deliver thee from the way of the evil man, from the man that speaketh froward things ;* 13. *Who leave the paths of uprightness, to walk in the ways of darkness ;* 14. *Who rejoice to do evil, and delight in the frowardness of the wicked ;* 15. *Whose ways are crooked, and they froward in their paths.*

The various snares for the young, about to be detailed, furnish a fearful picture of the temptations to which our children are exposed. Will it not awaken our earnest cries for their deep and solid conversion to God ; that *wisdom may indeed enter into their hearts,* and its *pleasures* be really enjoyed ; that they may have a religious taste, as well as a religious education ; that they may know the Gospel, not only in the

conviction of their conscience, or the excitement of their feelings, but
in the entire renewal of their hearts before God ?   This, and nothing
less, will preserve them from the snare of their cruel foe.   Every town
and village swarms with his emissaries ; first, initiated themselves into
the mysteries of his art ; then, going forth, laborious and practised
teachers, well instructed for his murderous work.   Against one of these
enticements we have been before warned. (Chap. i. 10–13.)   Another
is here given : The tempter bears his character upon his lips ; *the evil
man that speaketh proud things* against God and his law ; like a poisonous
fountain sending up poisoned waters.   Oh ! how quickly does the contamination spread !   He does not sin in ignorance.   He and his companions*° have probably been trained in *the paths of uprightness.* Having
come in contact with the pestilential breath of the ungodly, they have
caught the contagion, and eagerly spread it.   Readily do they *leave the
paths*, which they never heartily loved, *to walk in the ways of darkness,*
which their hearts do love. (Chap. iv. 16, 17. Job, xxiv. 13–16. John,
iii. 19, 20.)   Having left the hated paths, they become therefore fore-
most in iniquity.   Poisoned themselves, they would poison all around
them.   They *rejoice*, like Satan himself, *to do evil :*† to draw their
fellow-sinners into the net : and they *delight in those*, who are most
froward in their *wickedness.*‡   Thus they plunge deeper and deeper
into sin, till they lose all traces of the straight way, and all their *ways
become crooked*, leading with sure steps to eternal ruin.   Is not this the
picture, drawn to the very life, of many a Sunday-scholar, or a child of
godly parents, the subject of deep and tender care ; " hardened through
the deceitfulness of sin " (Heb. iii. 13), the neglect of faithful warning,
the stifling of solemn conviction ?   How do they deserve to be left of
God, who have first left him with such fearful aggravation !   Young
man ! especially shun companions, who are sinning against better
knowledge and instruction.   They are hardened in devotedness to
their master's work.   Oh ! if misguided sinners could but see sin in its
horrid deformity and certain end, would not " their hearts meditate
terror ? "   But *the crookedness of their ways* hides the end from view.
Satan presents the bait, palliates the sin, covers the enormity, closes
the eyes, and conceals the certain end of all — Hell. (Ps. cxxv. 5.
Rom. vi. 21 ; with 2 Cor. iv. 3, 4.)   *The froward in their paths* cannot
— will not — turn back.

16. *To deliver thee from the strange woman, from the stranger, which flattereth with her lips :* 17. *Which forsaketh the guide of her youth, and
forgetteth the covenant of her God.*   18. *For her house inclineth unto*

* The change to the plural number (*the man — who leave*) implies confederacy.
† Comp. Isa. iii. 9 ; Jer xi. 15. God's heavy judgment. 2 Thess. ii. 12.
‡ The sin of the heathen, Rom. i. 32.

death, and her paths unto the dead. 19. *None that go unto her return again : neither take they hold of the paths of life.*

Another snare of the fowler is here graphically pourtrayed.[*] *Wisdom hidden in the heart* is, as before, the most effectual *deliverance ;* restraining even the eye from the hurtful object.[†] Ought not the *strange woman,* even if she be born and baptized in a Christian land, to be counted as *a stranger*[‡] and foreigner among us ? One who had *forsaken the guide of her youth,*[§] and forgotten the solemn bond of *the covenant of her God*[||] —what else could she be to the unwary but a vile *flatterer with her lips ?* (Chap. v. 3 ; vii. 5, 21.) The slave of unlawful desire ; having no *guide* but her own will ; no pleasure but sensual gratification ; quickly she becomes her own and her victim's murderer. Her house is the land of death. (Chap. v. 5.) Eternal death is her doom. (Gal. v. 19–21. Eph. v. 5. Rev. xxi. 8 ; xxii. 15.) *Her paths incline to the dead,* with the awful monuments of Divine vengeance in olden time.[¶] Some instances indeed of *deliverance* are given ; not so much examples, as *special miracles,* of grace, to show how far the " arm of the Lord" can reach.[**] But so rare are they, that it is as if scarcely *none*[††] *that go unto her return again.* And what madness is it to rush into the snare upon so faint and glimmering hope of escape ! (Eccles. vii. 26.) The spell of lust palsies the grasp, by which its victim might have *taken hold of the paths of life* for *deliverance.* He that is " saved, is so as by fire" (1 Cor. iii. 15), the wonder of heaven and earth. " Is not this a brand plucked out of the fire ? " (Zech. iii. 2.)

20. *That thou mayest walk in the way of good men, and keep the path of the righteous :* 21. *For the upright shall dwell in the land, and the perfect shall remain in it ;* 22. *But the wicked shall be cut off from the earth, and the transgressors shall be rooted out of it.*

Here is the consummating blessing of *engrafted wisdom.* Not only

* Chap. v. 3–20 ; vi. 24 ; vii. 5–23 ; xxii. 14 ; xxiii. 27. Some commentators give an allegorical interpretation to these pictures, as descriptive of idolatry or false doctrine. ' But surely,' as Holden well observes, ' if there be any dependence to be placed upon the language of the sacred writer, any propriety in his expressions, it is to be understood in its literal sense, as a warning against the seduction of harlots. The spirit of allegorical interpretation may make the Scriptures speak whatever is prompted by the wildest fancy, or the deepest fanaticism.'—HOLDEN *in loco.* Comp. SCOTT *in loco.*
† Comp. Job. xxxi. 1, and our Lord's rule :—Matt. v. 28.
‡ *The strange woman—a stranger.* Two different words in the Hebrew, the latter appearing to mark a foreigner. Comp. Deut. xxiii. 17 ; Lev. xix. 29. It is, however, but too evident that this abandoned class was not confined to foreigners. Comp. Gen. xxxviii. 15, 16 ; Judg. xi. 1 ; 1 Kings, iii. 16.
§ Though an harlot, she might be (Chap. vii. 5, 10, 19) or might have been (John, iv. 17, 18) a married woman.
|| Mal. ii. 14–16. Comp. Ezra, xvi. 59, 60. Does not this sacred view of the marriage ordinance rebuke the legislative sanction which has now degraded it to a mere civil contract ?
¶ ' The dead.'—SCOTT and Bishop PATRICK *in loco.* Comp. chap. ix. 18. Heb. MEDE's *Learned Discourse,* vii.
** Solomon's own case. Comp. Luke, vii. 37–50 ; 1 Cor. vi. 9–11.
†† None in comparison, very few. Comp. Isa. lix. 4 ; lxiv. 7.

does it *deliver from evil men;* but it guides us *into the way of good men.*
Clad with this Divine armour, thou shalt have courage, like Joseph, to
turn thy face from the enchantment of Sin (Gen. xxxix. 9, 10), *and keep
the paths of the righteous,* rugged indeed, yet the only paths of rest and
security. (Cant. i. 7, 8. Jer. vi. 16.)   Thus shalt thou *dwell and remain
in the land,* as its original inheritor (Ps. xxxvii. 9, 11, 22, 29, 34.   Matt.
v. 5); having the best portion in earth, and an infinitely better portion
in heaven; while *the wicked and transgressors,* though they may "enjoy
the pleasures of sin for a season," shall be ultimately *cut off, rooted out,*
and "driven away" into everlasting ruin. (Chap. x. 30; xiv. 32; xv. 25.
Ps. lii. 5–7; xcii. 7. Matt. iii. 10.)

And now, what serious reader of this chapter can fail to estimate
above all price the privilege of being early enlisted under the banner
of the cross; early taught in the ways, and disciplined in the school, of
the Bible; and early led to hide that blessed book in the heart, as the
rule of life, the principle of holiness, the guide to heaven!

Parents, sponsors, teachers of youth; ponder your deep responsibility with unceasing prayer for special grace and wisdom.   Beware
of glossing over sins with amiable or palliating terms.   Let young
people be always led to look upon vicious habits with horror, as the
most appalling evil.   Discipline their vehemence of feeling, and all ill-
regulated excitement.   Keep out of sight, *as far as may be,* books calculated to inflame the imagination.   To give an impulse to the glowing
passion may stimulate the rising corruption to the most malignant
fruitfulness.   Oh! what wisdom is needed to guide, to repress, to bring
forth, develope safely, and to improve fully, the mind, energies, and sen-
sibilities of youth!

Young man! beware!   Do not flatter thyself for a moment, that
God will ever wink at your sinful passions; that he will allow for them,
as slips and foibles of youth.   They are the "cords of your own sins,"
which, if the power of God's grace break them not in time, will "hold"
you for eternity. (Chap. v. 22.)   Shun then the society of sin, as the
infection of the plague.   Keep thy distance from it, as from the pit of
destruction.   Store thy mind with the preservative of heavenly wisdom.
Cultivate the taste for purer pleasures.   Listen to the fatherly, pleading
remonstrance, inviting thee to thy rest—"Wilt thou not from this
time cry unto me, 'My Father! thou art the guide of my youth?'"
(Jer. iii. 4.)

CHAPTER III.

1. *My son, forget not my law; but let thine heart keep my commandments;*
   2. *For length of days, long life, and peace shall they add to thee.*

THIS is not the stern language of command.   It is our Father's voice
in all the endearing persuasiveness of promise—*My son*—He had
before instructed us to *seek and search* after wisdom, and set out before
us its invaluable blessings.   Now he calls us to bring it into practical
exercise—*Forget not my law.*   The wilful forgetfulness of the heart
(Chap. ii. 17. Ps. ix. 17 ; x. 4 ; comp. chap. iv. 5 ; Deut. iv. 23 ; Ps.
cxix. 93, 176), not the infirmity of the memory (for which a special,
though we fear too much neglected, help, is provided) (John, xiv. 26)
is here implied.   *Let thine heart,* like the ark of the testimony, be *the
keeping-place of my commandments.* (Chap. iv. 4. Deut. xi. 18. Isa. li. 7 ;
with Ezek. xi. 20. Heb. ix. 4.)   And is not this the child's desire—" O
that my ways were directed to keep thy statutes ?" (Ps. cxix. 6 ; comp.
verses 69, 129), while his conscious helplessness takes hold of the covenant promise—" I will put my law in their inward parts, and write it
in their hearts." (Jer. xxxi. 33.)

Indeed no laws, but God's, bind the heart.   All acceptable obedience
begins here.   The heart is the first thing that wanders from God : the
first also that returns.   Here is the vital principle. (Chap. iv. 23. Rom.
vi. 17.)   All religion without it is a mere name ; and, however the
professor may practise a thousand arts to put life into it, all must fail,
" The root being as rottenness, the blossom goes up as the dust."
(Isa. v. 24.)   If every moment were filled up with deeds of benevolence,
or external piety ; yet, except *the heart* was quickened to *keep the commandments,* the voice of rebuke would be heard—" Who hath required
this at your hand ?" (Isa. i. 11, 12.)   " The inner man's delight"
(Rom. vii. 22) stamps the excellency upon the service.   And this pleasure and perseverance in duty flow from a gracious change upon the
heart. (See Ezek. xi. 19 ; xxxvi. 26, 27.)

Herein also lies our interest, not less than our obligation.   The
reward of this *hearty* obedience (need we add—a reward of grace ?) is
a long and happy life—the highest earthly good. (Ps. xxxiv. 12 ;
comp. verse 16 ; iv. 10 ; ix. 11 ; x. 27 ; Job, x. 12.)   The wicked indeed
live long, and the godly often " live out only half their days."   The
wicked die in outward comfort ; the righteous in outward trouble.
(Eccles. ix. 2.)   But *length of days* is the promise to the righteous ;
whether for earth or for heaven, as their Father deems fittest for them.
In itself the promise, as regards this life, has no charm.   To the un-

godly it is a curse (Gen. iv. 11–15. Isa. lxv. 20) ; to the people of God
a trial of faith and patience (Gen. xxvii. 46 ; xlvii. 9. 1 Kings, xix. 4.
Job, vii. 16. Philip. i. 23, 24. Rev. xxii. 20) ; to all a weariness. (Chap.
xv. 15. Ps. xc. 10. Eccles. xii. 1.)   But *peace added* forms the sunshine
of the toilsome way (Ps. cxix. 165. Isa. xxxii. 17 ; xlviii. 17, 18) :
" peace with God through the blood of sprinkling" (Rom. v. 1. Eph. ii.
13, 14. Col. i. 20) ; eternal peace in his home and in his bosom (Ps.
xxxvii. 37. Isa. lvii. 2) ; where all the fightings of a rebellious flesh,
all the counter-strivings of a perverse and ungovernable will, shall have
ceased for ever.   " *Blessed are they that do his commandments*, that they
might have right to the *tree* of life, and may enter in through the gate
into the city." (Rev. xxii. 14.)

3. *Let not mercy and truth forsake thee ; bind them about thy neck ; write*
   them upon the table of thine heart ; 4. So shalt thou find favour and
   good understanding (marg., success,) *in the sight of God and man.*

Mercy and truth are the glorious perfections of God ; always in combined exercise (Gen. xxxii. 10. Ps. xxv. 10 ; lxxxv. 10 ; lxxxix. 14 ; c. 5 ;
cxvii. 2. Mic. vii. 18–20) for his people's good.   While we rest upon
them for salvation, let us copy them in our profession.   Are not his
children new-created in his image ?   Let then our Father's image be
manifested in us, " as his dear children." (Eph. iv. 24 ; v. 1, 2, 8.)   Let
these graces be, as with God, in combination.   'The want of one
buries the commendation of the other.   Such a one is a *merciful* man to
the poor ; but there is no *truth* in him.   Such a one is very just in his
dealings, but as hard as flint.'*   " Put on, as the elect of God, bowels
of *mercy*.   But lie not one to another.   Speak every man *truth* with
his neighbour." (Col. iii. 12, with 9. Eph. iv. 25.)   Indeed, ' as a rich
sparkling diamond added both value and lustre to a golden ring ; so do
these virtues of justice and mercy, well attempered, bring a rich addi-
tion of glory to the crowns of the greatest monarchs.'†
    But these virtues must not be in temporary or occasional exercise.
Let them not forsake thee.   Bind them as jewels *about thy neck.* (Chap.
vi. 21 ; vii. 3. Deut. vi. 8.)   Let them be " *written*, not in tables of
stone, but in fleshly tables of the heart." (Chap. vii. 3. 2 Cor. iii. 3.)
God indeed is not thy debtor ; yet none shall serve him for nought.
The man who shows *mercy* to his neighbour shall find it with him.
(Ps. xviii. 25. Matt. v. 7.)   " They that deal truly are his delight."
(Chap. xii. 22.)   So shalt *thou find favour and good understanding* (Ps.
cxi. 10) — (success) (Josh. i. 7, 8.   M. R.) — both *in his sight, and in*
the sight of man.   Witness Joseph in Egypt (Gen. xxxix. 2–4, 21–23 ;

---

* F. TAYLOR's *Comment on Chap.* i.-ix. ; 4to. 1655-1657.
† Bishop SANDERSON's *Sermon on Chap.* xxiv. 10-12.

xli. 37–43; xlv. 16); David in the family of Saul (1 Sam. xviii. 5, 14–16); the servants of God in the eastern courts;* the early Christians with the people around them. (Acts, ii. 44–47.)   What is more lovely than thus to live down reproach by consistent godliness?   What more acceptable to God, or more edifying to the Church ? (Rom. xiv. 16–19.) The Scripture connects the favour of God with the favour of men, as if the one was often the fruit of the other. (Comp. chap. xvi. 7.)   Such was the record of the holy child. (Luke, ii. 52.)   The highest crown of a youthful profession is conformity to this Divine pattern. (Comp. 1 Sam. ii. 26.)

5. *Trust in the Lord with all thine heart, and lean not to thine own understanding.   6. In all thy ways acknowledge him, and he shall direct thy paths.*

This is the polar-star of a child of God — faith in his Father's providence, promises, and grace.   The unmeaning expression of *trust* on the lips of the ignorant and ungodly is a fearful delusion.   What ground of confidence can there be when there is everything to fear? Can the sinner's God — a just, avenging God — be an object of *trust?* What owe we to that precious atonement, which has opened up our way to a reconciled God (Rom. v. 11), and assured our confidence in him as our Friend and Counsellor !   Nor is this the cold assent of the enlightened judgment.   It is the *trust of the heart, of all the heart.*   It is a child-like, unwavering (Ps. lxxviii. 2 Chron. xiv. 11. Contrast Jer. i. 6–8) confidence in our Father's well-proved wisdom, faithfulness, and love.   Any limit to this confidence is a heinous provocation. (Ps. lxxviii. 18–21.)   He is truth itself.   Therefore he would have us take him at his word, and prove his word to the utmost extent of his power.

But our *trust* must not only be *entire:* it must be *exclusive.*   No other confidence, no confidence in the flesh, can consist with it. (Comp. Philip. iii. 3.)   Man with all his pride feels that he wants something to *lean to.*   As a fallen being, he naturally *leans to himself,* to his own foolish notions and false fancies.   Human power is his idol.   His *understanding* is his God.   Many would rather be convicted of want of principle than want of talent.   Many bring God's truth to their own bar, and cavil at it, as an excuse for rejecting it.   In these and other ways, man " trusteth to himself, and his heart departeth from the Lord." (Jer. xvii. 5.)   This is the history of the fall; the history of man from the fall; the dominant sin of every unhumbled heart; the lamented and resisted sin of every child of God.   Need we advert to it as the sin of youth ?   How rare is the sight of the " younger submitting unto the elder !" (1 Pet. v. 5.)   If advice is asked, is it not with the hope of

* Dan. i. 8, 9; iv. 8, 9; v. 11; vi. 1–3, 27, 28. — His three companions, iii. 30; Ezra, vii. 9–12. Neh. ii. 1–6.   Mordecai, Esth. x. 3.

confirming a previously-formed purpose? In case of a contrary judgment, the young man's *own understanding* usually decides the course.

Great reason then is there for the warning—*Lean not to thine own
understanding*. Once, indeed, it gave clear unclouded light, as man's
high prerogative, "created in the image of God." (Gen. i. 26. Col.
iii. 10.) But now, degraded as it is by the fall (Ps. xlix. 20), and
darkened by the corruption of the heart (Eph. iv. 18), it must be a false
guide. Even in a prophet of God it proved a mistaken counsellor.
(2 Sam. vii. 2–5.) Yet though we refuse *to lean to it*, to follow it may
be implicit *trust in the Lord;* because it is a trust in his Divine power,
enlightening it, as his lamp for our direction. The Christian on his
knees, as if he cast his understanding away, confesses himself utterly
unable to guide his path. But see him in his active life. He carefully
improves his mind. He conscientiously follows its dictates. Thus
practical faith strengthens, not destroys, its power; invigorates, not
supersedes, exertion. (Comp. Gen. xxxii. 9–20; Neh. ii. 4–20; iv. 9.)

It is therefore our plain duty not to neglect *our understanding*, but
to cultivate it diligently in all its faculties. In a world of such extended knowledge, ignorance is the fruit of sloth, dissipation, or misguided delusion. But *lean not to thine understanding*. *Lean—trust in
the Lord*. Self-dependence is folly (Chap. xxviii. 26), rebellion (Jer.
ii. 13; ix. 23), ruin. (Gen. iii. 5, 6. Isa. xlvii. 10, 11.) 'The great
folly of man in trials'—as Dr. Owen justly remarks—' is *leaning to or
upon his own understanding* and counsels. What is the issue of it?
Whenever in our trials we consult our own understandings, hearken to
self-reasonings, though they seem to be good, and tending to our preservation; yet the principle of living by faith is stifled, and we shall in
the issue be cast down by our own counsels.'[o]

*Next—let our confidence be uniform—In all thy ways acknowledge
him.* Take one step at a time, every step under Divine warrant and
direction. (Comp. Ezek. viii. 21–23; Neh. i. 11.) Ever plan for yourself in simple dependence on God.[†] It is nothing less than self-idolatry
to conceive that we can carry on even the ordinary matters of the day
without his counsel. He loves to be consulted. Therefore take all thy
difficulties to be resolved by him. Be in the habit of going to him *in
the first place*—before self-will, self-pleasing,[‡] self-wisdom, human
friends, convenience, expediency. Before any of these have been consulted go to God at once. Consider no circumstances too clear to need
his direction.[§] *In all thy ways*, small as well as great; in all thy con-

---

* *Treatise on Temptation*, chap. viii. Comp. Job, xviii. 7; Hos. x. 8.
† Jam. iv. 15. *If the Lord will*—as Fuller remarks with his pithy quaintness—'a
parenthesis, and yet the most important part of the sentence.'
‡ See the awful hypocrisy, and judgment of asking counsel of God under this deadly
influence. Jer. xlii. 1–3, 19–22. Ezek. xiv. 1–6.
§ See the evil consequence of this inconsiderate neglect. Jos. ix. 14.

cerns, personal or relative, temporal or eternal, let him be supreme. Who of us has not found the unspeakable " peace" of bringing to God matters too minute or individual to be entrusted to the most confidential ear ? ° Abraham thus *acknowledged God.* Wheresoever he pitched a tent for himself there was always an altar for God. (Gen. xii. 7 ; xiii. 18.) In choosing a wife for his son there was a singular absence of world-liness. No mention was made of riches, honour, beauty ; only of what concerned the name and honour of his God. (Gen. xxiv. 1–8. Comp. also his servant, verse 12–27.) Thus did the wise man's father *in all his ways acknowledge God,* asking counsel of him in all his difficulties, and never disappointed.†

Now if we be weaned from the idolatry of making our bosom our oracle, and our heart our counsellor ; if in true poverty of spirit we go every morning to our Lord, as knowing not how to guide ourselves for this day ; our eye constantly looking upward for *direction* (Ps. v. 3 ; cxliii. 8–10 ; xxv. 4, 5), the light will come down.‡ *He shall direct thy paths.* We want no new revelations or visible tokens. (Such as Exod. xiii. 21, 22.) Study the word with prayer. Mark the Divine Spirit shedding light upon it. Compare it with the observation of the pro-vidences of the day (Ps. cvii. 43) ; not judging by constitutional bias (a most doubtful interpreter), but pondering with sober, practical, reverential faith. Let the will be kept in a quiet, subdued, cheerful readiness, to move, stay, retreat, turn to the right hand or to the left, at the Lord's bidding ; always remembering that is best which is least our own doing, and that a pliable spirit ever secures the needful guidance. (Comp. Ps. xxxii. 8, 9 ; Isa. xlviii. 17, 18, with xxx. 21.) We may " be led," for the exercise of our faith, " in a way that we know not" (Isa. xlii. 16 ; l. 10)—perhaps a way of disappointment, or even *of mistake.* Yet no step well prayed over will bring ultimate regret. Though the promise will not render us infallible ; our very error will be overruled for deeper humiliation and self-knowledge ; and thus even this myste-rious *direction* will in the end be gratefully acknowledged, " He led me forth in the right way." (Ps. cvii. 7.)

7. *Be not wise in thine own eyes : fear the Lord, and depart from evil ;*
   8. *It shall be health to thy navel, and marrow to thy bones.*

This warning against self-confidence is closely connected with the preceding verse. The *wise in his own eyes* is he, that *leans to his own*

° Phil. iv. 6, 7. "*In every thing.*"
† 1 Sam. xxiii. 9–11 ; xxx. 6–8. 2 Sam. ii. 1 ; v. 19. Comp. the smarting rod from the neglect of this godly habit. 1 Sam. xxvii. 1, with xxix.
‡ Matt. vi. 22. Comp. Ps. xxxii. 8 ; xxxiv. 5. Neh. i. 4–11 ; ii. 4–8. Sir M. Hale left it on record, when nearly eighty years old, as his experience, that whenever he had com-mitted his way simply and unreservedly to the Lord, he had always *directed his path.*

understanding.° Such wisdom is folly and self-delusion.† Put it away, and let it be thy wisdom to *fear the Lord, and depart from evil.* How striking is this connexion between *the fear of God* and the fear of sin. (Chap. xiv. 27 ; xvi. 6. Gen. xxxix. 9, 10. Neh. v. 15. Job, xxviii. 28.) Where God is honoured, sin is hated, loathed, and resisted. (Rom. vii. 18–24.) It lives indeed ; but it is condemned to die. (Ibid. vi. 6.) It cleaves to the child of God ; but his heart *departs from it.* Often is it the cause of the sickness of the body :‡ always of the soul. (Hos. vii. 9.) *The departure from it* in the exercise of self-denial and godly discipline, is *health* to the body. (Verses 1, 2.) The soul, drooping under the baneful influence of spiritual disease, revives in fruitfulness. (Hos. xiv. 5–7.) The man that *feareth the Lord*, under " the healing beams of the Sun of Righteousness, goeth forth " (Mal. iv. 2), as from his sick chamber, full of life and Christian energy. "The joy of the Lord is his strength." (Neh. viii. 10.)

9. *Honour the Lord with thy substance, and with the first-fruits of all thine increase ;* 10. *So shall thy barns be filled with plenty, and thy presses shall burst out with new wine.*

This rule of sacrifice is a costly precept to the worldling and the formalist.   But to the servant of God, is it not a privilege to lay aside a portion of *substance* with this sacred stamp,—"This is for God?" (1 Cor. xvi. 2.)   *The first-fruits of the increase* were the acknowledgment of redemption from Egypt. (Exod. xiii. 12, 13. Deut. xxvi. 1–10.) And shall we, redeemed from sin, Satan, death, and hell, deny the claim ? (1 Cor. vi. 19, 20.)   'Well, may we think *our substance* due, where we owe ourselves.'§   Nay, could we be happy in spending that *substance* on ourselves, which he has given us wherewith *to honour* him ? (Luke, xix. 13. Contrast xii. 16–22.)   What a value, what a dignity, does it give to the talent, that he should condescend to employ it for his own grand, eternal purposes !   This sacred devotedness is, moreover, the true road to riches. (Chap. xi. 24.)   God challenges us to " prove him now herewith," if the abundant harvest, and the overflowing vintage, shall not put unbelief and covetousness to shame. (Mal. iii. 10. 2 Chron. xxxi. 5–10.)   A niggardly spirit is, therefore, narrow policy ; contracting the harvest, by sparing the seed-corn. (2 Cor. ix. 6.   Hag. i. 4–6.)

---

* Verse 5. Comp. xxiii. 4. Rom. xii. 3-16. See the mind of God expressed in that solemn woe. (Isa. v. 21.)
† Even a heathen could remark —'I suppose that many might have attained to wisdom, had they not thought they had already attained it.' SENECA, *de Ira*, Lib. iii. c. 36. Comp. 1 Cor. viii. 2 ; Gal. vi. 3. 'Our knowledge should hold the light before us, and help us for the better discovery of our ignorance, and so dispose us to humility, not pride.'—Bp. SAN-DERSON'S *Sermon on Rom.* xiv. 3.
‡ In sensual indulgence—Chap. v. 8-11. Intemperance—xxiii. 29, 30. As a judicial infliction — Ps. xxxii. 3, 4 ; xxxviii. 1-8. 1 Cor. xi. 30.
§ Bishop Hall.

There is no presumption, or enthusiasm in looking for the literal fulfilment of the promise. If we doubt the temporal, should we not suspect our assumed confidence in the spiritual, engagements? For if the Lord's word be insufficient security for *our substance:* much more must it be for the infinitely weightier deposit of our soul!

The rule and obligation are therefore clear. The law dealt with us as children, and prescribed the exact amount. The gospel treats us as men, and leaves it to circumstance, principle, and conscience. This consecration of substance, as the seed-corn for the harvest, is as strange to the world, as would be the casting of the seed in the earth to an untutored savage. Yet is the result secure in both cases; only with this difference, that the temper of the earthly sower has no influence on the harvest; whereas the fruitfulness of the spiritual harvest mainly depends upon the principles of the work. Most important is it to beware of bye-ends and selfish principles; that we *honour the Lord*, not ourselves. Let there be a self-renouncing spirit (1 Chron. xxix. 14–16. Matt. vi. 1–4; xxv. 37–39), implicit faith (1 Kings, xvii. 12–16), constraining love (Rom. xii. 1. 2 Cor. v. 14, 15. Matt. x. 42), special regard to his own people. And doubt not, but he will affix his own seal—"Those that honour me, I will honour." (1 Sam. ii. 30. Comp. chap. xi. 25; xxii. 9; Heb. vi. 10.)

11. *My son, despise not the chastening of the Lord; neither be weary of his correction; 12. For whom the Lord loveth he correcteth; even as a father the son in whom he delighteth.*

Prosperity and adversity in their wise mixture and proportion, form our present condition. Each is equally fruitful in opportunity of *honouring the Lord;* in prosperity — by the full consecration of *our substance* (Verses 9, 10); in adversity — by a humble and cheerful submission to his dispensation. 'In prosperity it is well to expect the rod; and suppose it be his pleasure, let it not make thee either doubt of his gracious Providence, or out of impatience take any unlawful course to remove it from thee.'* His "exhortation"—the Apostle reminds us—"speaketh to us, as unto children."† And indeed, under no character does he approach so near to us, and endear himself so closely to us, as that of a Father Most precious at all times, especially under *correction*, is the privilege of adoption—*My son.*

Nowhere, indeed, are our corruptions so manifest, or our graces so shining, as under the rod. We need it as much as our daily bread. Children of God are still children of Adam; with Adam's will, pride,

* Bishop Patrick.
† Heb. xii. 5. We must not overlook the Apostle's testimony to the Divine inspiration of the Book; showing the instruction throughout to be the teaching of our Heavenly Father to his beloved children.

independence, and waywardness. And nothing more distinctly requires Divine teaching and grace, than how to preserve in our behaviour the just mean between hardness and despondency; *neither despising the chastening of the Lord, nor being weary of his correction.*

Too often, while we guard against an error on the right hand, we forget one not less hurtful on the left; like the man, who, in guarding against the precipice on the one side, rushes into some fearful hazard on the other. The middle path is the right path. *Doubtless the Lord means his chastening to be felt.* (2 Sam. xv. 26. Ps. xxxix. 10, 11.) A leviathan iron-heartedness (Job, xli. 24–29. Jer. v. 3) is the stubbornness of the flesh, not the triumph of the spirit; a frame most offensive to him, and most unseemly for the reception of his gracious discipline. To be as though no pain was felt or cared for; sullenly to "kick against the pricks" (Acts, ix. 5. Comp. chap. xix. 3), and to dare God to do his worst—this is, indeed, to *despise his chastening.*† But pride will lift up the head, stiff and unbending: many a stroke does it require to bring it down.

Yet, alas! this is not the sin only of the ungodly. Often do we see the child of God in an undutiful spirit (Job, v. 17. Heb. xii. 6), caring little whether his Father smiles or frowns. The *chastening* is lightly passed over. He considers only second causes, or immediate instruments. (Amos, iii. 6.) He is irritated by looking at the rod, rather than at the hand that inflicts it. (2 Chron. xvi. 10–12.) He shrinks from searching into the cause. He disregards his Father's loving voice and purpose. Hence there is no softening humiliation (Ps. xxxii. 3, 4); no "acceptance of the punishment of iniquity" (Lev. xxvi. 41, 43); no child-like submission; no exercise of faith in looking for support. Is not this to *despise the chastening of the Lord?*

But while some *despise* the hand of God as light, others "faint" under it as heavy. (Heb. xii. 5. Ps. xxxviii. 2, 3; xxxix. 10.) They are *weary of his correction.* Beware of yielding to heartless despondency, or fretful impatience. (Ps. lxxiii. 14; lxxvii. 7–10.) Resist hard and dishonourable thoughts of God. (Gen. xlii. 36. Judg. vi. 13. Jonah, iv. 9.) Their very admission spreads destruction. Very apt are we to judge amiss of our Father's dealings;‡ to neglect present duty; to cherish a morbid brooding over our sorrows (Job, vi. 1–16): to forget our title and privilege of adoption (Heb. xii. 5); or in obstinate grief to "refuse to be comforted" with the "hope of the end" (Ps. lxxvii. 2.

---

* The philosopher's definition is striking and accurate, but infinitely above his own practical standard—'Non sentire mala tua, non est hominis; et non ferre, non est viri.'—(It is inhuman not to feel thine afflictions, and unmanly not to bear them.)—SENECA, *Consol. ad Polyb.* c. 36.

† Comp. Pharaoh — Exod. vii. 23. Jehoram—2 Kings, vi. 31. Ahaz—2 Chron. xxviii. 22. Israel—Isa. i. 5. Zeph. iii. 2. Comp. Job, xv. 25, 26.

‡ Chap xxiv. 10. Isa. xl. 27–31; Comp. 1 Sam. xxvii. 1; 1 Kings, xix. 4; Job iii. 1–3; Jer. xx. 14-18.

Comp. Jer. xxix. 11 ; xxxi. 15–17.) And is not this to be *weary of his correction ?*

But these rules imply much more than their negative meaning. Instead of *despising*, reverence *the chastening of the Lord.* Let it be a solemn remembrance to thee, that thou art under thy Father's *correction.* (Lam. iii. 28, 29. Mic. vii. 9.) Receive it then in good part. Instead of being *weary* of it, hang upon his chastening hand, and pour thy very soul into his bosom. (1 Sam. i. 10–15.) Kiss the rod. (Job, xxxiv. 31, 32. 1 Pet. v. 6.) Acknowledge its humbling, but enriching, benefit. (Ps. cxix. 67–71.) Expect a richer blessing from sustaining grace, than from the removal of the deprecated affliction. (2 Cor. xii. 7–10.)

After all we must add, that chastening is a trial to the flesh (Heb. xii. 11) ; yet overruled by wonder-working wisdom and faithfulness to an end above and contrary to its nature. This very rod was sent in love to the soul. Perhaps we were living at ease, or in heartless back-sliding. The awakening voice called us to our Bible and to prayer. Thus eyeing God in it, we see it to be love, not wrath ; receiving, not casting out. We might perhaps have wished it a little altered ; that the weight had been shifted, and the cross a little smoothed, where it pressed upon the shoulder. But now that our views are cleared, we discern blessing enough to swallow up the most poignant smart. We see the " needs-be," for our preservation from imminent danger (Comp. Chap. i. 32 ; Ps. lv. 19), and for " the trial of our faith." We come to an unhesitating verdict in favour of the absolute perfection of the dispensation. (Ps. li. 4 ; cxix. 75.) Faith understands the reasons of the discipline (1 Pet. i. 6, 7) ; acknowledges it as a part of his gracious providence (Deut. viii. 2, 15, 16), and the provision of his everlasting covenant (Ps. lxxxix. 30–32) ; waits to see the end of the Lord (Jam. v. 11) ; and meanwhile draws its main support from the seal of adoption.

For indeed it is the declared test of our legitimacy. (Heb. xii. 7, 8. Rev. iii. 19.) He *corrects whom he loves, the son in whom he delighteth.* His discipline is that of the family ; not of the school ; much less of the prison. He corrects his children, not as criminals, but as those whom he beholds without spot, " made accepted in the Beloved." (Eph. i. 6.) Nor is there caprice, as too often with an earthly father, in his chastise-ment. (Heb. xii. 10.) It is wisdom in the spirit of love. " He rejoiceth over his child to do him good" (Jer. xxxii. 41) ; yet as a wise and affectionate father, he would not suffer him to be ruined for want of *correction.* (Chap. xiii. 24. Deut. viii. 5.) It is correction—this is for your humbling. It is only correction—this is your consolation. The intolerable sting of penal infliction is removed. Here then the child has rest indeed ?° The rod is now meekly, yea—thankfully borne, because it is in the hand of One supreme in wisdom, as in love,

---

° 1 Sam. iii. 18 2 Sam. xv. 25 ; xvi. 10, 11. Ps. xxxix. 9. Job, i. 21. Isa. xxix. 8.

who knows what is our need, and how to apply the discipline. He chooses the fittest time (Isa. xxx. 18. 1 Pet. v. 6), the surest yet gentlest means, the most considerate measure (Isa. xxvii. 7, 8. Jer. xxx. 11. Lam. iii. 31–33), the most effective instruments. And, comparing our affliction with our sin, is not the marvel that it is so light? (Ezra, ix. 13. Ps. ciii. 10. Lam. iii. 39.) Have we not more than deserved it all? 'I love the rod of my heavenly Father'—exclaimed the saintly Fletcher—' How gentle are the stripes I feel! How heavy those I deserve!'* 'O God, I have made an ill use of thy mercies, if I have not learnt to be content with thy *correction.*' †

Should he then at any dark season ask—"If it be so, why am I thus?" (Gen. xxv. 22)—you are thus, because this is your Father's training discipline for heaven.‡ He loves thee so well, that he will bestow all pains upon thee. He will melt thee in his furnace, that he may stamp thee with his image. (Isa. xxvii. 9; xlviii. 10. Zech. xiii. 9. Mal. iii. 3.) He would make thee "partake of his holiness" (Heb. xii. 10), that thou mightest partake of his happiness. But unless thou enter into his mind, thou wilt, so far as thou canst, defeat his purpose, and lose the benefit—a loss never to be told? (Comp. Jer. vi. 8.) Look then well into the dispensation. (Job, x. 2. Ps. cxxxix. 23, 24. Eccles. vii. 14. Lam. iii. 40.) Every rod is thy Father's messenger; and he will not bear to have his messenger *despised*. Be anxious to "hear the rod, and who hath appointed it" (Mic. vi. 9); well knowing that "the Lord hath not done without cause all that he hath done." (Ezek. xiv. 23.) Be more concerned to have it sanctified than removed; yea, above all things deprecate its removal, until it has fully wrought its appointed work. (Isa. iv. 4.) We can but admire that considerate dispensation, which uses these "*light*" afflictions as the means of deliverance from the most deadly evil. Should flesh and blood rebel; should the earthly tabernacle shake with "the blow of his hand" (Ps. xxxix. 10, ut supra): yet shalt thou bless him throughout eternity, that even by this crushing discipline he should accomplish his most merciful purpose. Meanwhile, give him unlimited confidence; and if some steps of the way are hid, wait and "see the end." (Job, xxiii. 8–10; Jam. v. 11.) Watch for the first whispers of his will, the first intimation of his Providence, the guidance of his eye. (Ps. xxxii. 8, 9.) Many a stroke will thus be saved to thy peace and quietness. This indeed is a golden opportunity, requiring for its due improvement much study, prayer, and retirement. No communion is so close, so endearing, so fruitful, as with a *chastening* God. Never is Christ more precious to

Comp. John, xviii. 11. The heathen philosopher has accurately drawn the line—'Chastisement is on the sufferer's account. Vengeance is for the satisfaction of him that inflicts it.' —ARIST. *de Rhetor* b. i. c. 10.
    * Life of Rev. H. Venn, pp. 238, 584.   † Bishop Hall.
    ‡ Job, xxxiii. 14–29; xxxvi. 8–10. Heb. xii. 7, 8, ut supra.—The term refers to the education of children.

us ; his love never more sweet, than in the midst,—yea, in the very form, of *chastening*. Never have we so full a manifestation of the Divine character (Ps. cxix. 75), and perfections. What we have before learnt in theory, we here learn experimentally ; and what we have before imperfectly understood, is here more fully revealed.° With regard to the full weight and duration of the trial, and all its minute circumstances, successively so bitter and piercing — we may ask — 'Which of them could be spared?' It is quite clear as to the whole time, the whole weight, the whole number and variety of circumstances that all and each were as necessary as any part. Where could we have stopped, without making that stop fatal to the great end? What does it all mean, but the Lord holding to his determination to save us ; all the thoughts of his heart, every exercise of his power, centering in this purpose of his sovereign mercy?

13. *Happy is the man that findeth wisdom, and the man that getteth* (marg. draweth out), *understanding ;* 14. *For the merchandize of it is better than the merchandize of silver, and the gain thereof than fine gold ;* 15. *She is more precious than rubies, and all the things thou canst desire are not to be compared to her.*

Who does not admire this glowing picture of happiness? † The wisdom of this world affords no such happiness. (Eccles. i. 18.) Yet cold and barren is admiration, without an interest in the blessing. The *happy man has found* a treasure, where possibly he least expected it, under *the chastening of the Lord*. David ‡ and Manasseh (2 Chron. xxxiii. 12, 13) found (as who hath not found?) 'God's house of correction to be a school of instruction.'§ Under all circumstances, however, prayerful diligence in the search of *wisdom* ensures success. (Chap. ii. 1–6.) The naturally wise man is a fool in heavenly *wisdom*. The man of prayer *getteth understanding, draweth it out* to light, as out of the hid treasure.‖ We wonder not at the merchant-man's concentrated interest, at his untiring toil.¶. Here the wise man, himself enriched with *the*

* Job, xlii. 5. Comp. the Apostle's most instructive and encouraging exposition. Heb. xii. There is some slight variation between Heb. xii. 6, and verse 12. The one describes the mode and subject of *the chastening*. The other shows the Father's delight in his chastened child. Some by inverting the first clause, ver. 12, grossly pervert the meaning, and conclude themselves to be the Lord's children, *because they are afflicted*. But though every child is corrected, not every one that is corrected is a child. The same hand—but not the same character—gives the stroke, to the godly and the ungodly. The scourge of the Judge is widely different from the rod of the Father. Comp. 1 Sam. xxviii. 15-20, with 2 Sam. xii. 13, 14 ; Chap. i. 26. Isa. i. 24, with Jer. xxxi. 18-20. Hos. xi. 7. 8 ; also Isa. xxvii. 7-9. Nor is it *chastening*, but the *endurance of chastening*, according to the rules prescribed, that seals our adoption. Heb. xii. 7

† *Happy man.*—Heb. plural. Comp. Ps. i. 1 ; xxxii. 1. Blessedness—to mark supreme and perfect happiness. See the beautiful description of Wisdom, Ecclus. xxiv. 1-19.

‡ Ps. cxix. 67, 71. Hence he commends it, Ps. xciv. 12.

§ TRAPP, *in loco*.

‖ M. R. Comp. Chap. viii. 35. M. R. Chap. ii. 4. Matt. xiii. 44.

¶ Impiger extremos currit mercator ad Indos,
Per mare pauperiem fugiens, per saxa, per ignes.
HOR. *Epis.* i. 1. 45.

merchandize of fine gold (1 Kings, ix. 26–28) points out to us a *better merchandize.* It is the search for "the pearl of great price," *more precious than rubies, yea, than all things that could be desired.** So the Apostle judged. So upon a trial he found it. All the world's show, all his former valuable "gain, he counted as dung and dross" for "the true wisdom"—"the excellency of the knowledge of Christ Jesus his Lord." (Philip. iii. 4–8.) Never will solid happiness be known without this singleness of judgment and purpose. This inestimable blessing must have the throne. The waverer and the half-seeker fall short. Determined perseverance wins the prize. (Philip. iii. 12–14.)

16. *Length of days is in her right hand, and in her left hand riches and honour;* 17. *Her ways are ways of pleasantness, and all her paths are peace;* 18. *She is a tree of life to them that lay hold upon her: and happy is every one that retaineth her.*

Behold this heavenly Queen dispensing her blessings! *Her right hand* presents the promise of both worlds (Verse 2. Ps. xci. 16. 1 Tim. vi. 8)—the rich enjoyment of the world's lawful comforts (1 Tim. vi. 17), and the yet higher joy of serving the Lord and his church—a privilege for which the Apostle was content for a while to be detained from heaven. (Philip. i. 23, 24.) Add *length of days* for eternity to the balance; and the amount sets at nought all computation. *Her left hand* offers *riches and honour,*† so far as may be for her children's good; yet in their highest splendour, only a faint shadow of her more "durable *riches,*" and of the *honour* of a heavenly crown.

But what say we of *her ways?* Is she a sullen matron, who entertains her followers only on sighs and tears; so that to obtain the joys of the next life, we must bid eternal adieu to the contents of this life; 'we must never more expect a cheerful hour, a clear day, a bright thought to shine upon us?'‡ This is the world's creed—a slander of the great forger of lies, to deter us from *wisdom's ways.* They must be *ways of pleasantness,* because "Thus saith the Lord." And if we feel them not to be so, we know them not.

The man of pleasure utterly mistakes both his object and his pursuit. The only happiness worth seeking is found here; that which will live in all circumstances, and abide the ceaseless changes of this mortal life. *The ways* may be dark and lonely; yet how does the sunshine of reconciliation beam upon their entrance! Every step is lighted from above, and strewed with promises; a step in happiness, a step to heaven.

---

* Matt. xiii. 45, 46, with Chap. xxiii. 23. Comp. Chap. viii. 11, 19; Job, xxviii. 15–18. Most truly does the great Moralist define Wisdom to be 'The knowledge of the most honourable things'—ἐπιστημη των τιμιωτατων.—ARIST. *Ethic* b. vi. chap. vii.

† See the treasures of *right and left hand* promised to the wise man himself, 1 Kings, iii. 12–14.

‡ BISHOP HOPKINS' *Works,* iv 354, 355.

Wisdom's work is its own reward (Ps. xix. 11. Isa. xxxii. 17)—strictness without bondage. (Matt. xi. 29, 30.) God rules children, not slaves. They work neither from compulsion, nor for hire ; but from an ingenuous principle of gratitude to their Benefactor ; filial delight in their Father. *Pleasant* therefore must be the labour—yea—the sacrifices—of love ; short the path ; cheerful the way, when the heart goes freely in it.

It is saying far too little, that the trials of *these ways* are not inconsistent with their *pleasantness*. They are the very principles of the most elevated pleasure. 'The verdict of Christ,'—says Dr. South—'makes the discipline of self-denial and the cross—those terrible blows to flesh and blood—the indispensable requisite to the being his disciples.'* And yet, paradoxical as it may appear, in this deep gloom is the sunshine of joy. For if our natural will be "enmity to God" (Rom. viii. 7), it must be the enemy to our own happiness. Our pleasure, therefore, must be to deny, not to indulge it ; to mortify sinful appetites, that only "bring forth fruit unto death." (Ib. vii. 5.) Even what may be called the austerities of godliness are more joyous than "the pleasures of sin." Far better to cross the will, than to wound the conscience. The very chains of Christ are glorious. (Acts, v. 41, 42 ; xvi. 24, 25.) Moses endured not "his reproach" as a trial. He "esteemed it as a treasure—greater riches than the treasures of Egypt." (Heb. xi. 26.) Our principles are never more consoling than when we are making a sacrifice for them. Hannah yielded up her dearest earthly joy. But did she sink under the trial? Did she grudge the sacrifice? "Hannah prayed and said—*My heart rejoiceth in the Lord*" (1 Sam. i. 26 ; ii. 1) ; while—to show that none serve him for nought—for one child that was resigned, five were added. (Ib. ii. 20, 21.)

In fact, the world have no just conception of the real character of *wisdom's ways*. Religion to them is associated with cold, heartless forms and irksome restraints—much to do, but nothing to enjoy. But they only see half the prospect. They see what religion takes away. But they see not what it gives. They cannot discern, that, while it denies sinful, it abounds in spiritual, pleasures. We drudge in the ways of sin. But we "shall sing in the ways of the Lord." (Isa. lvii. 10 ; with Ps. cxxxviii. 5.) Here is the only thing below worth the name of joy — solid — abiding — overflowing — satisfying (Hab. iii. 18)—God's own joy. (John, xv. 11 ; xvii. 13.) It is not a mere impulse of vapid sentimentalism, but a principle of Christian energy, invigorating for duty, supporting for trial. (Neh. viii. 10.) Here, then, "we have less toil, and reap more fruit." For will not any reasonable man, upon the hearing of the names of the things only, presently yield, that "love, joy, peace, and gentleness," which are "fruits of the Spirit," are far more lovely, more easy, fuller of sweetness and calmness, less vexatious, than

* *Sermons*, vol. i. Matt. xvi. 24.

are " hatreds, emulations, murders," and those other " works of the flesh ? " °

But *ways of pleasantness* are not always safe. Yet *all wisdom's paths are peace.* The deadly breach is healed. The cloud vanishes. Heaven smiles. And *peace,* the Saviour's last bequest, is realised even in the heat of " this world's tribulation." (John, xvi. 33.) " The feet are shod " for the rugged path " with the preparation of the Gospel of peace." (Eph. vi. 15 ; with Deut. xxxiii. 25.) The subjugation of the will, the sorrow of contrition, the weariness of the cross — all end in peace. (Ps. xxxvii. 37. Isa. lvii. 2, with 20, 21.)

Yet nothing can make *wisdom's ways* palatable to a carnal mind. " They that are after the flesh do mind the things of the flesh ; " so that, as " they cannot please God," God's ways cannot please them. (Rom. viii. 5, 8.) Nor again — though *wisdom's ways are ways of pleasantness,* are wisdom's children always happy. Sometimes a naturally morose temper gives a gloomy tinge to religion. Professors forget, that it is no matter of option, whether they should be happy or not ; that it is their obligation no less than their privilege to be so ; that the commands of God on this duty † carry weight, and demand obedience. The prophets in the burst of their rapture search heaven and earth, bring forth the most beautiful objects of nature ; nay — call the inanimate creation into glowing sympathy with the joys of the Gospel. (Ps. xcvi. 11–13 ; xcviii. Isa. xliv. 23 ; lv. 12, 13.) A rejoicing spirit is the character of the servants of God (Phil. iii. 3. Acts, ii. 46, 47), specially in affliction. (2 Cor. vi. 10 ; viii. 2. 1 Pet. i. 6–8.) Is then thy happiness clouded ? Has there not been some deviation from *wisdom's paths ?* Thy God calls thee to search, to humble thyself, to return. (Jer. ii. 17–19. Hos. v. 15 ; vi. 1.)

Lastly — to the glory, beauty, and fruitfulness of wisdom, the Paradise of God alone can furnish the full counterpart. (Rev. ii. 7.) '*The tree of life* was the means ordained of God for the preservation of lasting life, and continual vigour and health, before man sinned. So true wisdom maintains man in the spiritual life of God's grace, and the communion of his Spirit.'‡ Once our way was barred up, and none could touch her. (Gen. iii. 22–24.) Now our way is opened to her in a better paradise. (Heb. x. 19–22.) We " sit down under her shadow with great delight." Her branches bend down upon this world of sin and misery. Her clusters hang within the reach of the youngest child, and " the fruit is sweet to the taste " (Cant. ii. 3) ; sweeter than ever man tasted, since he became an exile from Eden. For what is so refreshing, as near communion with God ; access to him ; boldness in

---

* Bishop SANDERSON's *Sermon on Gal.* v. 22, 23.
† Such as Ps. xxxii. 11 ; xxxvii. 4. Phil. iv. 4. 1 Thess. v. 16. Comp. the warning, Deut. xxviii. 47, 48.   ‡ Diodati.

his presence; admission to his most holy delights? And if the earthly shadow and fruit be so rich, what will be "on the other side of the river,"—her monthly fruits, her healing leaves! (Rev. xxii. 2.) And yet only the weeping, wrestling soul can *lay hold upon* the beloved object (Gen. xxxii. 26–28. Hos. xii. 3, 4), and embrace it, in despite of all the enemy's struggle to loosen the grasp. (Matt. xi. 12.) And even, when Almighty power has enabled us to *lay hold*, the same continual miracle of grace, the same continually-renewed effort of faith, is needed to *retain it.* (1 Tim. vi. 12.) There must be "continuance in the ways" (Isa. lxiv. 5. John, viii. 31); "settled, rooted, and grounded" (Col. i. 23; ii. 7); "keeping the works;" holding the beginning of our confidence steadfast "unto the end." (Rev. ii. 26. Heb. iii. 6, 14.) *Happy is every one that retaineth her.* The promises are "to him that overcometh." (Rev. ii. iii.) God honours perseverance in the weakest saint.

This lovely description of wisdom's blessing is no fancy picture, but Divine reality. Rest not, till thine heart is filled with its substance. Take it to the Lord in prayer; and ere long, thou shalt rejoice in thy portion.

19. *The Lord by wisdom hath founded the earth : by understanding hath he established* (marg. prepared) *the heavens.* 20. *By his knowledge the depths are broken up, and the clouds drop down the dew.*

We have seen *wisdom*, as it is in man, with all its enriching blessings. Here we behold its majesty, as it is in the bosom of God, and gloriously displayed in his works. 'Hereby he showeth, that this wisdom, whereof he speaketh, was everlasting, because it was before all creatures; and that all things, even the whole world, were made by it.'✢ Behold it *founding the earth* "upon nothing;" and yet "so sure, that it cannot be moved." (Job, xxvi. 7. Ps. xciii. 1.) See how this great Architect *hath established the heavens*, fixing all their bright luminaries in their respective orbits (Gen. i. 14–16. Ps. cxxxvi. 5. Jer. x. 12; li. 15)—'such a glorious canopy set with such sparkling diamonds!'† Each of these departments declares his *knowledge*—In the earth, by *breaking up the depths*, and gathering them up into rivers and streams for the refreshment of man. (Chap. viii. 24–29. Gen. i. 9, 10. Job, xxxviii. 8–12. Ps. civ. 8–13)—*In the heavens*, by collecting the moisture into *dew*, and dropping down fatness upon the parched ground;‡ each of these countless drops falling from this Fountain of life. (Job, xxxviii. 28.) Thus does every particle of the universe glitter with infinite skill. (Ps. civ. 24.) The earth is its pavement, and the

✢ Reformers' Notes. † Leighton's beautiful fragment on Ps. viii. Works, vol. ii.
‡ Gen. xxvii 28, 29. There is a philosophical difficulty in supposing "*the clouds* to drop down the dew," which is the moisture rising from the lower region, sometimes a very few feet from the earth. In the East, however, the dew is said to fall from a considerable height. Gesenius states, that the Hebrew word represents a 'gentle rain.'

heavens—its ceiling ; both miracles of wisdom, to " declare the glory of God." (Ps. xix. 1.)   How beautiful is the uniformity of the two great systems of God !   Both are the work of the same Architect.   Both display the *wisdom and knowledge* of God. (John, i. 1–14. Eph. i. 8 ; iii. 10. Col. i. 13–17.)   The universe is a parable, a mirror of the gospel. The manifestation of these Divine Perfections in the field of Creation opens a rich provision for our happiness.   Much more let their more glorious exhibition in the great work of redemption fill us with adoring praise —" O the depth of the riches, both of *the wisdom and knowledge* of God !"[*]

21. *My son, let them not depart from thine eyes : keep sound wisdom and discretion :* 22. *So shall they be life unto thy soul, and grace unto thy neck.*

Again we listen to Wisdom's voice.   Her repetitions are not " vain repetitions ; " but well fitted to impress upon youth (Isa. xxviii. 9, 10) the weight of her instructions. (Philip. iii. 1. 2 Pet. i. 12.)   As thy much-loved treasure, as thy daily guide — *let them not depart from thine eyes.* (Chap. vii. 1–3.)   Worse than valueless are they, if received as notions ; of inestimable price, if *kept* as principles.   God's teaching is *sound wisdom* (Deut. iv. 9 : vi. 8. Josh. i. 7, 8) ; full of light and substance ; transfiguring Divine truth with heavenly glory.   Therefore *keep* it close to thine heart.   Exercise it in that practical *discretion,* which disciplines all our tempers and duties.   Man's wisdom is utterly devoid of all energy.   The soul, " alienated from the life of God " (Eph. iv. 18), is in a state of death, until " the entrance of God's word giveth light and understanding " (Ps. cxix. 130) —" the light of life." (John, viii. 12.)   " The excellency of this knowledge is, that," " with this light and understanding," it giveth *life* to them that have it. (Eccles. vii. 12.   Comp. Chap iv. 22 ; vi. 23.)   Every truth under its influence springs up into the new creature with heavenly glow, and with all *the grace* of " the beauty of the Lord ; "[†] outshining, even in the most despised garb, the richest glory of an earthly crown.

23. *Then shalt thou walk in thy way safely, and thy foot shall not stumble.*
    24. *When thou liest down, thou shalt not be afraid : yea, thou shalt lie*

---

[*] Rom. xi. 33.   Full of profound thought are the words of our admirable Hooker— 'That which moveth God to work is Goodness ; that which ordereth his work is Wisdom ; that which perfecteth his work is Power.   All things, which God in these times and seasons hath brought forth, were eternally and before all time in God ; as a work unbegun is in the artificer, which afterwards bringeth it into effect.   Therefore whatsoever we do behold now in this present world, it was enwrapped within the bowels of Divine Mercy, written in the book of Eternal Wisdom, and held in the hands of Omnipotent Power, the first foundations of the earth being as yet unlaid.   So that all things which God hath made are in that respect the Offspring of God.   They are in him, as effects in their highest cause.   He likewise is actually in them ; the assistance and influence of his Deity is their life.'—Book v. lvi. 5.

[†] Ps. xc. 17 ; cxlix. 4.   Comp. Chap. i. 9.   'Grace to thy jaws'—is the Douay Version, with the Marg. Explanation — ' Merit for the words of thy mouth.'

down, and thy sleep shall be sweet. 25. *Be not afraid of sudden fear, neither of the desolation of the wicked, when it cometh.* 26. *For the Lord shall be thy confidence, and shall keep thy foot from being taken.*

The habitual eyeing of the word keeps the feet in a slippery path. (Chap. iv. 11, 12. Ps. xvii. 4 ; xxxvii. 23 ; cxix. 9, 11, 133.) David, from inattention to wisdom's words, "well-nigh slipped." (Ps. lxxiii. 2–17.) Peter from the same neglect fearfully *stumbled.* (Matt. xxvi. 33–35, 69–75.) But our sleeping hours, no less than our waking steps, are divinely guarded. "So he giveth his beloved sleep." (Ps. cxxvii. 2. Comp. cxxi. 3, 4.) "Underneath them are the everlasting arms." (Deut. xxxiii. 27. Comp. Lev. xxvi. 6.) They enjoy a child-like repose, sleeping in his bosom without fear. Thus did David 'sleep in God, and in a state of salvation,' amid the tumultuous warfare with his undutiful son.* Peter in prison, in chains, between two soldiers, on the eve of his probable execution, when "there seemed but a step between him and death"—Yet in such a place, in such company, at such a moment, did *he lie down so fearless, and sleep so sweetly ;* that even the shining light failed to disturb him, and an angel's stroke was needed to awaken him.† What would not many in troublous times, waking at every stir, give for one night of this *sweet sleep !* And yet how many such nights have we enjoyed ; waking, as Jacob on his stony—we might add—downy, pillar, in the consciousness of our Father's keeping ! But where has been our renewed dedication to God? (Gen. xxviii. 11, 18–22.)

But *sudden fear* may come. Yet *be not afraid.* (Job, v. 21–24. Comp. 2 Kings, vi. 16, 17 ; Jer. xxxix. 15–18.) It is *the desolation of the wicked.* They must fear. (Isa. lvii. 20, 21.) Child of God! run you to your *confidence,* and "be safe." (Chap. xiv. 26 ; xviii. 10. Isa. xxvi. 1, 20.) Surely *he shall keep thy foot from being taken.* (Ps. xci. 1–3.) Noah found this security in the flood of the ungodly ; Lot in the destruction of Sodom (2 Pet. ii. 5–9) ; the Christians in Pella, in *the desolation of the wicked city.* Luther sung his song of *confidence*—"God is our refuge and strength." (Ps. xlvi.) In the consummating *desolation, when it cometh*—what will then be the *sudden fear*—the undismayed *confidence ?* "All the-tribes of the earth will mourn" at the sight of their despised Saviour—then their Judge. (Chap. i. 27. Luke, xxi. 26. Rev. i. 7 ; vi. 15–17.) But, "when ye see these things, then look up, and lift up your heads, for your redemption draweth nigh." (Luke, xxi. 28. Comp. 2 Thess. i. 7–10.)

---

* 'Obdormit in Deo, et in statu salutis.'—*Lyra.*—Ps. iii iv. 8. Compare the beautiful picture, Ezek. xxxiv. 25-28, in contrast with chap. iv. 16. Deut. xxviii. 66.

† Acts, xii. 6, 7. Our Martyrologist records of John Rogers, the proto-martyr in the Marian persecution, that 'on the morning of his execution, being found fast asleep, *scarce with much shogging could he be awaked.*'—FOXE, vi. 699.

27. *Withhold not good from them to whom it is due* (the owners thereof, marg.), *when it is in the power of thine hand to do it.* 28. *Say not unto thy neighbour, Go, and come again, and to-morrow I will give; when thou hast it by thee.*

The wise man now comes to practical points. He shows the fruit of selfishness—*withholding dues.* Many are the forms of this dishonesty—borrowing without payment (Ps. xxxvii. 21), evading the taxes; "keeping back the labourer's hire." (Jam. v. 4. Jer. xxii. 13–17. Comp. Gen. xxxi. 7 ; Deut. xxiv. 14, 15.) But the rule probes deeper than this surface. If we have no legal debt to any, we have a Gospel debt to all. (Rom. xiii. 8.) Even the poor is bound by this universal law to his poorer neighbour. (Eph. iv. 28. Comp. 2 Cor. viii. 1–3.) Every one has a claim upon our love. (Comp. Luke, x. 29–37.) Every opportunity of doing good is our call to do so. Our neighbours are the real *owners of our good.* (Marg.) The Lord of all has transferred his right to them, with a special reference to "his own brethren." (Gal. vi. 10. Mark, ix. 41. Matt. xxv. 31–40.) Kindness is therefore a matter, not of option, but of obligation ; an act of justice no less than of mercy. Not indeed that it may be demanded by our fellow-men. But the obligation lies upon conscience ; and to *withhold the due* will be our eternal condemnation. (Matt. xxv. 41–45. Comp. Deut. xxiii. 3, 4.)

Christian benevolence will also do good in the kindest manner. Delay is an offence against the law of love. Too often the cold repulse —*Go, and come again*—is a cover for selfishness. There is a secret hope that the matter will be forgotten, dropped, or taken up by some other party. Often an application is put off from mere thoughtlessness. *We have it by us.*† But it does not just now suit our convenience. This is a serious injury to the applicant. A little given in time of need is more than a larger sum when the time is gone by. We should cultivate a quick sensibility of the wants and sufferings of others ; putting ourselves as much as possible in their place ; not only "doing good," but "*ready* to every good work." (Tit. iii. 1. 1 Tim. vi. 18.) If we are to "*do* justly"—which sometimes (as in the punishment of criminals) may be our sorrow ; we are like our gracious God (Mic. vii. 18), to *love* mercy (Ib. vi. 8. Comp. Rom. xii. 8 ; 2 Cor. ix. 7); seizing the present, perhaps the only (Chap. xxvii. 1. Gal. vi. 10), opportunity ; rather anticipating the need than wantonly or thoughtlessly delaying to relieve it. (2 Cor. viii. 10.) The Gospel presents every neighbour before us as a brother or sister needing our help, and to be loved and cared for "as ourselves." (Lev. xix. 18.) Why do we not more readily

* The example and admonition of Christ are evidently directed against this iniquity. Matt. xvii. 24–27 ; xxii. 15–21.

† See how Job rebutted his friend's accusation, xxii. 9, with xxxi. 16. Comp. Jam. ii. 15, 16.

acknowledge this standard? The Lord raise us from our selfishness, and mould us to his own image of mercy and love! *

29. *Devise not evil against thy neighbour, seeing he dwelleth securely by thee.*
30. *Strive not with a man without cause, if he have done thee no harm.*

The command—*withhold not good*—is naturally followed by the forbidding to do *evil*. The treachery here rebuked was a scandal even to a heathen.† It is generally abhorred by the world, and should be doubly hated by a godly man. With him all should be clear and open as the day. *An evil device against a neighbour*, from whatever cause, is a cursed sin. (Chap. vi. 14–18. Deut. xxvii. 24. Ps. xxxv. 20; lv. 20. Jer. xviii. 18–20.) But to take occasion from confidence reposed, betrays "the wisdom that descendeth not from above—devilish." (Jam. iii. 15.) Such was the craft of Jacob's sons against the unsuspecting Shechemites (Gen. xxxiv. 13–29; xlix. 5–7); Saul's malice against David, when under his protection (1 Sam. xviii. 22–26); Joab's murder of Abner and Amasa (2 Sam. iii. 27; xx. 9, 10); Ismael's of Gedaliah. (Jer. xli. 1, 2.) No trial cuts so keenly. (Ps. lv. 12–14.) This was one of the bitters in the Saviour's cup of suffering. (John, xiii. 21, with Ps. xli. 9; Matt. xxvi. 46–50). And many a wounded spirit has been cheered by his sympathy with this poignant sorrow. (Heb. iv. 15.)

Yet we must guard not only against secret malice, but against *causeless strivings*. A propensity to embroil ourselves in quarrels (Chap. xvii. 14; xviii. 6; xxv. 8, 9) kindles *strife*, instead of following the rule of peace. (Rom. xii. 18.) This spirit is a great hindrance to holiness (Heb. xii. 14. Col. iii. 12–15), and inconsistent with a true servant of God. (2 Tim. ii. 24.) Irritable persons strongly insist upon their rights, or what they conceive to be due to them from others. " Is there not"—say they—" a cause?" But impartial observers frequently judge it to be *striving without cause;* that no harm has been done; none at least to justify the breach of love; that more love on one hand, and more forbearance on the other, would have prevented the breach; that "there is utterly a fault—Why do ye not rather take wrong?" (1 Cor. vi. 1–7.) How valuable is a close application

---

* Dr. South's caustic application may be wholesome probing—" Was ever the hungry fed, or the naked clothed, with good looks or fair speeches? These are but thin garments to keep out the cold, and but a slender repast to conjure down the rage of a craving appetite. My enemy, perhaps, is ready to starve; and I tell him I am heartily glad to see him, and should be *very ready* to serve him. But still my hand is closed, and my purse shut. I neither bring him to my table, nor lodge him under my roof. He asks for bread, and I give him a compliment—a thing indeed not so hard as a stone, but altogether as dry. I treat him with art and outside, and lastly, at parting, with all the ceremonial of dearness, I shake him by the hand, but put nothing into it. I play with his distress, and dally with that which was not to be dallied with—want, and misery, and a clamorous necessity.'—*Sermon on Matt.* v. 44.

† 'Fallere eum, qui læsus non esset, nisi credidisset.'—CICERO *pro Roscio.*

of the self-denying law of Christ! (Such as Matt. v. 39–41.) How
earnestly should we seek from himself his own meek and loving spirit!
(1 Pet. ii. 21–23.) ' O Lord, pour into our hearts that most excellent
gift of charity, the very bond of peace, and of all virtues; without
which, whosoever liveth is counted dead before thee.'[*]

31. *Envy thou not the oppressor* (a man of violence, marg.) *and choose
none of his ways.* 32. *For the froward is an abomination to the Lord;
but his secret is with the righteous.*

What is there—we might ask—to *envy in the oppressor?* The love
of power is a ruling passion; and the slave of his own will enjoys a
brutish pleasure in tyranny. Yet little reason have we to envy him,
much less *to choose his ways.* (Chap. xxiv. 1. Eccles. iv. 1.) Can he
be happy, going *froward* in his way, in perverse contradiction to the
will of the Lord? with the frown of Heaven? ' For he who hateth
nothing that he hath made, abhors those who have thus marred themselves. They are not only abominable, but ' *an abomination* in his
sight.''† Really to be *envied,* or rather ardently to be desired, is the lot
of *the righteous,* enriched with the *secret of the Lord*—" his covenant and
fatherly affection, which is hid and *secret* from the world."‡ Sinners are
an abomination. Saints are his delight. ' They are God's friends, to
whom he familiarly imparts, as men used to do to their friends, his
mind and counsels, or his *secret* favour and comforts, to which other
men are strangers.'.§ Communion with himself (John, xiv. 21–23);
peace (Phil. iv. 6, 7); joy (Chap. xiv. 10); assurance (Rev. ii. 17);
teaching (Matt. xi. 25; xiii. 11–17; xvi. 17. John, vii. 17. 1 Cor. ii.
12, 15); confidence (John, xv. 15); an enlightened apprehension of
providence (Gen. xviii. 17, 18. Ps. cvii. 43); yea, all the blessings of
his covenant (Ps. xxv. 14)—this is *the secret* between God and the
soul, an enclosed portion, hidden from the world, sealed to his beloved
people. Here then — child of God — " dwell in the secret place of the
Most High." (Ib. xci. 1.) If he hath given to thee the knowledge of
himself, and of thine interest in him; and to *the froward oppressor* only
worldly advantage; is it not the seal of his love to thee, and rejection
of him? Is it not infinitely more to dwell on high with thy God, than
in the vain pomp of an ungodly world? (Ib. lxxxiv. 10.)

33. *The curse of the Lord is in the house of the wicked; but he blesseth the
habitation of the just.*

The contrast between the sinner and the saint, affects us not only

* Collect for Quinquagesima Sunday. 1 Cor. xiii. 4–7.
† HENRY *in loco*, chap. vi. 14–18; xi. 20; xv. 9. Mic. ii. 1, 2. See the Lord's open
judgment, Exod. ix. 16; xiv. 28. Isa. xxxvii. 21–38. Acts, xii. 1, 2, 23.
‡ Reformers' Notes.
§ POOL's *Annotations,* ' He loves them dearly as his intimate friends, to whom he com-
municates the very secrets of his heart.'—DIODATI.

personally, but relatively. *The curse or blessing of the Lord* follows us
to our homes. Shall we then envy *the wicked*, with his cup of earthly
joy filled to the brim? *The curse of the Lord is in his house* (Mal. ii. 2)
— a " curse that never cometh causeless." (Chap. xxvi. 2.) Let him
think — ' It is my Maker's curse — how awful, that my being and my
curse should come from the same sacred source ! ' It is not the impo-
tent *wishing* of ill. Could we trace its deadly work, we should see the
man wasting, withering, consuming under it. Observe " the roll in the
house of the thief, and of the swearer — twenty cubits long " — a long
catalogue of woes ; " flying "— to mark its swiftness ; " remaining in
the midst of the house ; consuming it even with the timbers and stones
thereof." (Zech. v. 1–4.) Is this an idle dream ? Surely — but for the
blindness of the heart, *the wicked* would see the naked sword hanging
by a hair over his head, or the awful " hand-writing upon the wall,"
solemnly proclaiming — " There is no peace — saith my God — unto
the wicked." (Dan. v. 5, 6. Isa. lvii. 21.) Vainly will the proud worm
resist. Ahab multiplied his *house* beyond all human average, as if to
set at defiance *the curse* pronounced against it. Yet at one stroke all
were swept away. (1 Kings, xxi. 20–22. 2 Kings, x. 1–11.) Similar
instances* abundantly prove whose words shall stand — man's or
God's. (Jer. xliv. 28.) " Who hath hardened himself against him, and
prospered ? Who hath resisted ,his will ? " (Job, ix. 4. Rom. ix. 19.)

But bright is the sunshine of *the just*. Not only *is the secret of the
Lord with their souls*, but *his blessing on their habitation*. And when he
blesseth, who can reverse it ? (Num. xxiii. 20. Job, xxxiv. 29.) Many
a homely cottage, tenanted by a child of Abraham, shines more splen-
didly than the princely palace of the ungodly.† An heir of glory
dwells here. A family altar of prayer and praise consecrates it as the
temple of Jehovah. (Gen. xii. 8.) Promises, like clouds of blessings,
rest over it. God has been honoured, and God will honour. (2 Sam.
vi. 11. Jer. xxxv. 18, 19. 2 Tim. i. 18.) " They that dwell under his
shadow shall return." (Hos. xiv. 7.) Is then my *house* under *the curse
or blessing of the Lord?* Let my God be honoured in his own gifts : that
I and mine may be manifestly sealed with the full tokens of his love.

34. *Surely he scorneth the scorners : but he giveth grace unto the lowly.*

Two Apostles have combined with the wise man, to set out this
rule of the Divine government.‡ On no point is the mind of God more
fully declared than against pride — the spirit of *scorning*. It displaces

---

* JEROBOAM : 1 Kings, xiv. 9–11 ; Amos, vii. 9. BAASHA : 1 Kings, xvi. 1–4, 12, 13.
JEHU : 2 Kings, xv. 8–12. Hos. i. 4. HAZAEL : Amos, i. 4. JEHOIAKIM : Jer. xxii. 13–19.
CONIAH : Ib. 24–30. ESAU : Obad 18. Comp. chap. xiv. 11 ; xv. 25.

† Job, xxix. 4. Isa. iv 5. Ενθα και οι Θεοι. ' The gods are within '— said the Heathen
philosopher of his poor cottage.—F. TAYLOR *in loco*.

‡ James, iv. 6. 1 Peter, v. 5.—The exact quotation of the LXX. save the substitution of

man, and would, if possible, displace God himself. Jealous therefore of
his own glory, he sets himself in battle array, as against the usurper of
his prerogative, the rebel against his dominion.° Witness the Babel-
builders (Gen. xi. 1–9); Pharaoh (Exod. xiv. 13); Sennacherib (Isa.
xxxvii. 33–38); the proud opposers of his Gospel (Ps. ii. 1–4)—all the
objects of *his scorn.* But most hateful to him is the sinner, that will not
submit to his righteousness, that *scorns* the corner-stone of salvation.
How fearfully does it then become " a rock of offence," of eternal ruin !
(Rom. x. 3, with ix. 32, 33. Matt. xxi. 41–44.) *Surely* without doubt,
without way of escape from his frown, *he scorneth the scorners.*

A *lowly* spirit—a deep conviction of utter nothingness and guilt—
is a most adorning grace. Nor is it an occasional or temporary feeling,
the result of some unexpected hateful disclosure, but an habit, " cloth-
ing " the man (1 Pet. v. 5) " from the sole of the foot to the head." It
combines the highest elevation of joy with the deepest abasement of
spirit. And those who sink the lowest, stand nearest to the most
exalted advancement. For " *he that scorneth the scorners, giveth grace to
the lowly*"—" more grace " (Jam. iv. 6), till his work is perfected in
them. ' He pours it out plentifully upon humble hearts. His sweet
dews and showers of grace slide off the mountains of pride, and fall on
the low valleys of humble hearts, and make them pleasant and fertile.'†
The centurion (Matt. viii. 5–10); the Canaanite (Ib. xv. 21–28); the
penitent (Luke, vii. 44–50); the publican (Ib. xviii. 13, 14); such as
these are the objects of his favour. (Isa. lxvi. 2.) Their hearts are his
dwelling-place. (Ib. lvii. 15.) Their inheritance is his kingdom.
(Matt. v. 3.) The soul, swelling with its proud fancies, has no room
for his humbling grace. Blessed exchange of the little idol of self-
esteem for Him; who alone has the right ! when even his own graces
are only desired, as instruments to set out his glory.

35. *The wise shall inherit glory : but shame shall be the promotion of fools,*
(exalteth the fools, marg.)

This is the last contrast drawn to restrain our envy at the prosperity
of the wicked. (Verse 31.) It carries us forward to the coming day,
when all shall " discern" in the full light of eternity. (Mal. iii. 18.) *The
wise—the heirs of glory*—are identified with *the lowly* (Verse 34 ; xi. 2)
—the heirs of grace. Self-knowledge—the principle of lowliness—
is the very substance of *wisdom.* Their inheritance also is one—*grace
and glory.* (Ps. lxxxiv. 11.) For what higher *glory* can there be than

---

Θεος for Κυριος. ' The Apostle's quotation of this passage, though somewhat different in
the words, is the same in the sense with the original. For *scorners* in Scripture are *proud,
insolent, wicked men.* And to resist such persons, by rendering their schemes abortive, and
by humbling them, is emphatically called *a scorning of them.*'—MACKNIGHT on James, iv. 6.
° αντιτασσιται, LXX.
† Leighton on 1 Pet. v. 5. Compare also on Chap. iii. 8.

the *grace,* which " hath redeemed" a vile worm of the earth, " and made him a king and priest unto God?" (Rev. v. 9, 10.) Oh! let the redeemed cherish honourable thoughts of their present *glory.* Be careful to clear it from the defilement and degradation of the world's dust, and enjoy it in adoring praise to Him, who hath chosen thee to this so undeserved grace. (Ib. i. 5, 6.)

But who can tell *the glory* of the after *inheritance*—not like this world's glory—the shadow of a name; but real, solid; ' an infinite gain, in the exchange of dross for down-weight of pure gold.'* All occasion of sin and temptation is shut out for ever. ' The tree of knowledge shall be without enclosure. There shall be neither lust, nor forbidden fruit; no withholding of desirable knowledge, nor affectation of undesirable. The glorified spirits touch nothing that can defile, and defile nothing they touch.' † But after all, the glory of this glory will be communion and likeness with our Lord—"to be with him—to behold his glory." (John, xvii. 24. 1 John, iii. 2.) We need not pry too minutely. Thus much is clear. The value of our inheritance is beyond all price; its happiness unspeakable; its security unchangeable; its duration eternity. *The wise shall inherit glory.* "They that be *wise* shall shine as the brightness of the firmament for ever and ever." (Dan. xii. 3. Matt. xiii. 43.)

Oh! will not the fools then discover the vanity of this world's glory, too late to make a wise choice? *Shame* is their present fruit. (Chap. xiii. 18; x. 9.) Honour even now sits unseemly upon them. (Chap. xxvi. 1.) But "what fruit will eternity bring" of those things, whereof they will "*then* be ashamed?" (Rom. vi. 21.) Truly *shame will be their promotion.* Their fame will be infamous, their disgrace conspicuous; lifting them up, like Haman upon his elevated gallows (Esther, vii. 9)—' a gazing-stock to the world.' How solemn and complete will be the great separation for eternity! " Many that sleep in the dust of the earth shall awake; *some to everlasting life, and some to shame and everlasting contempt.*" (Dan. xii. 2.)

CHAPTER IV.

1. *Hear, ye children, the instruction of a father, and attend to know understanding.* 2. *For I give you good doctrine, forsake ye not my law.*

SURELY these frequent repetitions are as the angel's visit to the prophet —"waking him, as a man that is wakened out of his sleep." (Zech. iv. 1.) A mind like Solomon's, "large even as the sand that is on the seashore" (1 Kings, iv. 29), might readily have made every sentence a

* Leighton on 1 Pet. v. 10.
† HOWE's *Blessedness of the Righteous.* Chap. v. xi.

fresh discovery of his knowledge. But more suitable to our sluggish and forgetful heart is "the word of the Lord, precept upon precept." (Isa. xxviii. 13.) Children are often bereft or destitute of a parental instructor. Here these orphans are taken up, and called to *hear the instruction of a father.* For truly does the wise man, like the Apostle in after days, "exhort and charge, *as a father doth his children."* (1 Thess. ii. 11.)

Solomon evidently speaks from the mouth of God, declaring his *doctrine* — his *law.* Therefore he claims *attention to know understanding, for I give you good doctrine.* (Eccles. xii. 9–11.) To many, exciting (Ezek. xxxiii. 31, 32), curious and speculative (2 Tim. iv. 3, 4), compromising (Isa. xxx. 10. Jer. v. 31), self-righteous, self-exalting doctrine (Gal. i. 6, 7), is more attractive. But — young people! — remember — that which humbles the soul before God ; that which exhibits the free grace of the Gospel ; which melts down the will, consecrates the heart, imbues with the spirit of the cross — however unpalatable to the flesh — is alone *good doctrine* for the soul. Therefore *forsake it not.* Do not be carried away with the senseless cry, — 'Everybody thinks contrary.' What is the judgment of the mass of mankind worth on the great subject of religion ? "This their way is their folly." This is God's stamp upon man's "saying," however applauded and "approved" by successive generations. (Ps. xlix. 13.) Shall this world's judgment be preferred to the word of God? "The morning" of the resurrection will reflect the glory of eternity upon the choice of the narrow path. (Ib. v. 14.)

3. *For I was my father's son, tender and only beloved in the sight of my mother. 4. He taught me also, and said unto me, Let thine heart retain my words: keep my commandments, and live. 5. Get wisdom, get understanding; forget it not; neither decline from the words of my mouth. 6. Forsake her not, and she shall preserve thee: love her, and she shall keep thee. 7. Wisdom is the principal thing; therefore get wisdom; and with all thy getting, get understanding. 8. Exalt her, and she shall promote thee: she shall bring thee to honour, when thou dost embrace her. 9. She shall give to thine head an ornament of grace; a crown of glory shall she deliver to thee.*

Solomon here claims our *attention* as a teacher of youth, on account of his own godly education by such a *father.* He was a *tender* child (1 Chron. xxii. 5 : xxix. 1), *well-beloved,* as an *only* son.* The more dearly he was loved, the more carefully was he *taught.* Thus we are brought into the family of "the man after God's heart," to hear him

---

* Not *really* the *only* son. 2 Sam. v. 14. 1 Chron. iii. 5. Thus Isaac was called the only son (*i. e.* most beloved). when Ishmael was another son: Gen. xxii. 2, 12, 16, with xvii. 19. So the Church is called "*the only one—the choice*"—implying others, out of which the choice was made. Cant. vi. 9.

" commanding his child" in the fear and service of the Lord. (Comp. also 1 Kings, ii. 2–4 ; 1 Chron. xxii. 6–16 ; xxviii. 9, 10, 20. Comp. Gen. xviii. 19. Deut. vi. 7.) A special mercy is it to us, if we can tell of an Abraham or a David—of a Lois or an Eunice, having *taught* and bound us to the ways of God ! (2 Tim. i. 5 ; iii. 14, 15.) Parents! remember, a child untaught will be a living shame. (Chap. xxix. 15.) Training discipline, not foolish indulgence, is the truest evidence of affection to our *tender and beloved* ones. (Chap. xiii. 24 ; with 1 Kings, i. 6.)

But let us examine this beautiful specimen of parental instruction.[*] *Observe the anxiety for his son's heart-religion. Let thine heart retain my words.* Often (and this is a comfort to a weak memory) *words* may be lost to the memory, yet practically *retained in the heart.* This *heart-keeping* is the path of life (Verse 13 ; vi. 23 ; viii. 34, 35. Isa. lv. 3. Zech. iii. 7), without which all is dead. Observe again *the extreme earnestness of the exhortation.* Many a parent, like Augustine's father,[†] insists—' Get wealth, worldly honour, or wisdom.' This godly parent inculcates " line upon line "— *Get* heavenly *wisdom ; get it with all thy getting*—at any cost and pains (Chap. xxiii. 23. Comp. 1 Kings, x. 1 ; Matt. xii. 42), as *the principal thing ;* and when thou hast got it —*forget it not*—decline not from it—forsake it not [‡]— *love* [§]— *embrace*— *exalt* — *her.* Such a *keeping* is she for thy soul ! (Chap. ii. 10–18.) Such a treasure for thy happiness ! Such a *promoting honour* even in this life ! Such an *ornament of grace* in the Church ! Such *a crown of glory* in heaven ! This is not the style of a cold pleader, enforcing with decent seriousness some unimportant truth. It is the father, feeling that his child's soul is perishing, unless it be taught and led in wisdom's ways. Parents! do we know this stirring concern, anxiously looking out for the first dawn of light upon our child's soul ? Do we eagerly point out to him *wisdom as the principal thing,* to be *gotten first ?* (Matt. vi. 33.) Is it our own first choice, infinitely above this world's glitter (1 Kings, iii. 5–12. Phil. iii. 7, 8) ; not only important, but all-important ? It can have no place, if it has not the first place. If it be anything, it will be everything. Earthly wisdom may be " a goodly pearl." But this " wisdom from above is the pearl of great price ; " worth *getting*

---

[*] Where David's instruction begins, is obvious. Where it ends, is not so clear—Whether it be ver. 6, 10, 12, or 13 ; or as F. Taylor asserts, at the close of the ninth chapter. But as Geier observes—' Let the reader form his own judgment ; provided that we pay due obedience to the instruction, it matters little, whether we have it in the words of David or Solomon.'

[†] Of whom he records—'This father of mine never troubled himself with any thought of— How I might improve myself towards thee, so that I proved eloquent, though I were withal left undrest by thy tillage '—*Confess.* ii. 3.

[‡] See the great importance of this continuance, John, viii. 30, 31. Col. i. 22, 23. Heb. iii. 6, 14, contrasted with Matt. xiii. 20, 21.

[§] Thus Jerome wrote to a friend —' Beg now for me, who am grey-headed, of the Lord, that I may have Wisdom for my companion, of which it is written—' Love her, and she shall keep thee.' "

indeed; but only to be *got*, by "selling all that we have, to buy it." (Matt. xiii. 45, 46.)

10. *Hear, O my son, and receive my sayings; and the years of thy life shall be many.* 11. *I have taught thee in the ways of wisdom; I have led thee in right paths.* 12. *When thou goest, thy steps shall not be straitened; and when thou runnest, thou shalt not stumble.* 13. *Take fast hold of instruction: let her not go: keep her; for she is thy life.*

It is instructive to see a king (whether David or Solomon) not forgetting in the midst of his royal cares his domestic responsibilities. We are told—'Youth will have its swing.' 'So'—adds an old Commentator solemnly—'it may—to hell.'* For where else can a wayward will lead? Let us see the need of guidance of every step, both to take and to avoid. *The ways of wisdom* assure a happy life in the favour of God. (1 Tim. iv. 8, with chap. iii. 1, 2. Ps. xxxiv. 12–14. 1 Pet. iii. 10–12.) And what rest to the parent's conscience on the deathbed will be the recollection of children, not brought up for the world, but *taught in these ways!* Yet this cannot be, if the rod, when needed, has been spared; if the will has been indulged; the love of the world cherished. *This will be*—if godly discipline has been exercised; if the Bible has been laid down as the rule of life; if habits of prayer, love to the service of God, fellowship with his people, have been encouraged. The path, though rough and sometimes lonely, is *a right path*, and a path of liberty. (Ps. cxix. 32, 45.) The single eye will preserve a steady walk. (Chap. x. 9. Isa. xlviii. 17, 18. Matt. vi. 22.) *Thou shalt run, and shalt not stumble.* (Chap. iii. 21–26. Hos. xiv. 9.)

And yet the animated exhortation *to take fast hold*, shows the struggle necessary to retain our principles. Feeble, indeed, is our *hold*, when connected *merely* with the excitement of novelty (Matt. xiii. 20, 21), temporary convictions (Ps. lxxviii. 34–36; cvi. 12, 13), the restraint of education (2 Chron. xii. 1; xxiv. 2. 15–18), unestablished knowledge (Gal. iii. 1–4), or the indulgence of sin. (Mark, vi. 18–26.) Truths received only in the understanding, not becoming the daily nourishment of the soul, never fix on the heart. *The fast hold of instruction* is by a personal living faith; including an intense interest, and persevering pursuit; "continuing in the things which we have heard and been assured of;" cleaving with purpose of heart unto the Lord. (2 Tim. iii. 14. Acts, xi. 23; ii. 42.) As Jacob detained the angel (Gen. xxxii. 26–29); as the spouse *held fast hold* of her Beloved (Cant. iii. 4); as the disciples "constrained the Saviour to abide with them" (Luke, xxiv. 28, 29)—So—young Christian—*let her not go, Keep her*, as the man "for joy" guarded his precious treasure. (Matt. xiii. 44.) So let thy heavenly treasure stand above every earthly blessing. Thus will

* Taylor.

it be *thy life.* (Chap. iii. 18. Eccles. vii. 12.)   And while others " turn
back, and walk no more " in the way, thine heart will turn to its only
spring of happiness—"Lord, to whom shall I go ? *Thou hast the words
of eternal life.*" (John, vi. 67–69.)

14. *Enter not into the path of the wicked, and go not in the way of evil men.*
   15. *Avoid it, pass not by it, turn from it, and pass away.*   16. *For
   they sleep not, except they have done mischief: and their sleep is taken
   away, unless they cause some to fall.*   17. *For they eat the bread of
   wickedness, and drink the wine of violence.*

How often does fellowship with *the wicked* loosen the *fast hold of
instruction!*   Their path is so contrary to the way of *instruction,* that
the very *entrance into it* is forsaking the way of God.   Their character
is here drawn in their Father's image—first sinners, then tempters.
Mischief is their meat and drink. (Job, xv. 16. Ps. xiv. 4.)   'To do
evil is more proper and natural than to sleep, eat or drink.'°   With
sleepless eagerness do they pursue their work (Job, xxiv. 15, 16. Ps.
xxxvi. 4. Mic. ii. 1), caring little for any lengths of *violence,* so that
they do mischief, or cause some to fall. (Chap. i. 10–14, 16; ii. 14; xxiv. 2.
Ps. x. 8. 2 Pet. ii. 14.) Judas with his midnight torches (John, xviii. 3);
the early morning assemblage of the Jewish rulers (Luke, xxii. 66); the
frenzied vow of the enemies of Paul;† and many a plot in after ages
against the Church—all vividly pourtray this unwearied wickedness.

Yet if we be preserved from this undisguised malignity, what are
all the allurements for every rank and circumstance of life, but the more
subtle poison of the murderer?   A light-minded young person pours
into his companion's ear—simple and inexperienced in the ways of
sin—perhaps filthy conversation; or presents before him images of
lasciviousness.   What but a rooted principle of grace can save his
unsuspecting victim?   Or again—the venomous infidel, intent upon
" spoiling " (Col. ii. 8) his fellow-creature of his most precious treasure,
drops into his bosom the repetition of the first lie. (Gen. iii. 4.)   No
principle appears to be given up, no fundamental doctrine denied; yet
the foundation of an unwavering confidence is shaken to pieces.   And
is not this *mischief and violence* as the murderer's stab?

Surely then it is mercy, that forbids needless intercourse with *the
evil man.* (Eph. v. 11.)   With a constitution prone to evil, when the
alternative is, whether we shall shun or dare the danger, can we doubt
our path?   The whole Scripture is on the side of caution, to hazard
nothing, except on a plain call of Providence.   'Because we are free,

* Reformers' Notes.
† Acts, xxiii. 12. Such a spirit is graphically described by the Classics :—
   Et si non aliqua nocuisses, mortuus esses. — Virgil, *Eclog.* iii. 15.
      Ergo non aliter poterit dormire ; quibusdam
      Somnum rixa facit. — Juvenal, *Sat.* iii. 278-282.

we may not run wild.'° Half our virtue we owe to being out of the way of temptation. Observe how the wise man heaps up his words— *Enter not into the path*—no—not so much as set thy foot into it. If some accident throws thee into it, *go not* on in it; *avoid it* with detestation.† *Pass not by it,* lest thou shouldest unwittingly turn in. (Chap. v. 8.) Not only *avoid* it when near, but avoid nearness to it. It is like living in the atmosphere of contagion, in the midst of virulent and fatal disease. The earnest repetition of the warning shows at once the imminency of the danger, and the certainty of the injury. The world around us is the action of mind upon mind. We are continually, through the medium of intercourse, moulding ourselves by other minds, and other minds by our own. Intercourse with the ungodly must, therefore, be fraught with fatal contamination. (1 Cor. xv. 33. Ps. cvi. 35. Chap. xxii. 24, 25.) The occasions, the company, the borders of temptation —all must be *avoided.* (Chap. ix. 10, 15. Gen. xxxi. 9, 10.)

Young people are apt to plead with those who have the charge of their best interests—'What harm is there in this or that path?' Apart from other evils—this is plain. It is a contagious atmosphere. You are drinking in poison. It is far more easy to shun the occasion of sin, than the sin when the occasion presents it; to resist the beginnings, than the progress, of sin. There must, therefore, be no tampering with it; no trial of strength, to see how far our resolutions will keep us. Let the examples of Lot (Gen. xiii. 10–13; xiv. 12), Dinah (Gen. xxxiv. 1, 2), Solomon (1 Kings, xi. 1–5), Peter (Matt. xxvi. 58, 69–74), warn us, how far only the *entrance into the path of the wicked* may carry us; lengths that we could never have contemplated in prospect without horror. It may appear an harmless outset. But how far on? The *entrance* is fatally connected with the next step onward. The frightful extent of the probability of falling might make the boldest tremble. Those at least, that know their own corruption and weakness, will shrink back, where you tread lightly. Here and there, indeed, there may be some special miracle of preservation. But no one comes out of *the path* without hurt (2 Chron. xviii. 1–3; xix. 2; xx. 35–37); and the general issue is an open door to ruin. To pretend to dread sin without fearing temptation, is self-delusion. Satan has too nearly allied them for us to separate them. The evil company is loved, then the evil of the company.‡ To pray " not to be led into tempta-

---

* Bishop HALL's *Contempl.* B. xv. 3. † LEIGH's *Critica Sacra.* See CARTWRIGHT.
‡ Eusebius mentions a young man, whom St. John committed to the special charge of the Bishop of Ephesus; but who by evil company was drawn away to be a captain of robbers, until St. John went after him, and brought him back. B. iii. c. 20. — Augustine's recollections of his youthful theft was—' By myself alone I would not have done it. It was the company that I loved, with whom I did it.' He adds —' O nimis iniqua amicitia!' When they said—' Come, let us go and do it, I was ashamed not to be as shameless as they.'— Confess. Lib. ii. 8, 9.

tion ;" yet not to " watch, that we enter not into it "— is practically to contradict our prayers ; to mock our God, by asking for what we do not heartily wish. " Walk then with God and with his people, separate from an ungodly world." (Chap. ix. 6. 2 Cor. vi. 17.) Yet do not presume upon safety, even in separation from the ungodly. The whole tempting world may be presented to your imagination. The unsearchable deceitfulness of the heart may bear fearfully upon you. The tempter may in solitude, as with our Lord, put forth his special power. (Matt. iv. 1.) Walk closely with God in secret, and he will spread his almighty covering over you for your security. *Avoid* fellowship with them, who hinder your fellowship with God. (Ps. cxix. 63, 114, 115, also xvii. 4 ; xxvi. 4, 5.)

18. *The path of the just is as the shining light, that shineth more and more unto the perfect day.*

This is a fine contrast of the Christian's *path* of light with the dark and dangerous *path of the wicked.* It is not the feeble wasting light of a taper, nor the momentary blaze of the meteor ; but the grand luminary of heaven, " coming out of his chamber, and rejoicing as a strong man to run his race " (Ps. xix. 5), from earliest dawn to his noon-day glory. And a beautiful sight it is, to see the Christian thus rising out of darkness ; not indeed with uniform brightness, but deepening from the first faint beginning of his course ; rising higher and higher ; widening his circle ; advancing onward with increasing brightness *unto the perfect day.* Knowledge, faith, love, holiness, irradiate every step. It is at first but a glimmering ray, the first dawn of day. He does not come at once into the " marvellous light." There is much — often long-continued — struggle with his own wisdom and self-righteousness. And even when brought to a simple dependence on the great work of Christ, it is long ere he sees the fitness and proportion of its several parts, providing for the honour of every perfection of God, as well as the supply of every want of man. Long also is it, ere he marks the just balance of promise and precept ; the sure connection between justification and sanctification ; the accurate arrangement, by which, while we are not saved by works, we cannot be saved without them ; and while we work of ourselves, our strength and trust is in another. Nor is it at the outset that we discern the identity of happiness with conformity to Christ, and find heaven in communion with God, and consecration to his service. Thus also, in the indistinct beginning of the course, sin lies within a narrow compass. It includes little besides the grosser enormities. Many things are thought harmless, which the spiritual law condemns. But as the line becomes more marked, old habits and associations, hitherto unsuspected, become convicted by a clearer light, and are ultimately relinquished. It is in this path that

as the Christian " follows on," the eye is more unveiled (Hos. vi. 3.
Comp. Mark, viii. 22–25), the heart more enlightened, the truth more
vividly impressed upon the conscience, the " understanding " more
quick in " the fear of the Lord," the taste more discerning between
good and evil.   Faith now becomes more strong in the Saviour's love,
more simple in the promises of God.

Obviously also love will increase as light expands.   In proportion
to knowledge of our sinfulness and ruin must be the gratitude for the
remedy.   The view of heaven — in proportion to the clearness of our
apprehension of it — must enlarge our love to him, who has obtained
our title to it.   Thus our knowledge converts itself into a motive,
expanding our love more widely to all the legitimate objects of it.   We
cannot, indeed, always compare its warmth at different periods.   But
knowledge and love, like the light and heat, must go together under
the beams of knowledge ; subjection to the Redeemer's sceptre becomes
more unreserved ; love rises to a higher estimation, to a closer union
with him, to a more intimate complacency in him.   Experience may
be confused.   But light will clear away the mists.   Practice in some
points may be inconsistent.   But the advances, however weak, will be
sure.   " Beholding as in a glass the glory of the Lord, we are changed
into his image from glory to glory, even as by the Spirit of the Lord."
(2 Cor. iii. 18. Job, xvii. 9. Ps. lxxxiv. 7.)   Such is the *path of the just.*
The devout Nathanael was cheered with the promise of a brighter day.
(John, i. 46–51.)   The clouds on the minds of the Apostles gradually
melted away before a brighter sun. (Mark, vi. 52 ; x. 35 ; xvi. 14, with
John, xvi. 13 ; Acts, ii.)   The Eunuch and Cornelius, sincerely seeking, rejoiced in the full sunshine of Gospel light. (Acts, viii. 27–39 ; x.)
The Thessalonian Church *shone more and more* with Christian graces.
(1 Thess. i. 3. 2 Thess. i. 3.)

But is this *shining light* the picture of my *path ?*   There is no command given — " Sun, stand thou still." (Josh. x. 12.)   Therefore it rebukes a stationary profession.   It is a rising and advancing, not a
declining, sun.   Therefore it rebukes a backsliding state.   It is not
necessary that every thing should be perfect at once.   There may be an
occasional cloud, or even (as in the cases of David and Peter) a temporary eclipse.   But when did the sun fail of carrying its early dawn *unto
perfect day ?*   Despise not, then, " the day of small things." (Zech. iv.
10.)   But be not satisfied with it.   Aim high, and you will reach nearer
the mark.   A fitful, fluctuating course, instead of illustrating this beautiful figure, throws around the profession a saddening uncertainty.
Religion must be a *shining* and progressive *light.*   We must not mistake the beginning for the end of the course.   We must not sit down
on the entry, and say to our soul — " Soul — take thine ease."   There
is no point, where we may repose with complacency, *as if there* were no

loftier heights, which it was our duty to climb. Christian perfection is the continual aiming at perfection. (See Phil. iii. 12–15.) Let us hasten on to *the perfect day,* when *the path of the just* shall be eternally consummated ; when 'they shall come to full perfection, which is — when they shall be joined to their Head in the heavens.'* "Then shall they shine forth as the sun in the kingdom of their Father." (Matt. xiii. 43.) And yet even here will not *the path* of eternity, no less than of time, be *shining more and more ?* Shall we not be exploring that unsearchable "height, and depth, and length, and breadth, that passeth knowledge," until we "be filled with all the fulness of God ?" (Eph. iii. 18, 19.) Will not light therefore be more glorious, and love more full of praise and adoration ? Yes, surely, the world of eternity will be one *perfect day* of ever-increasing light and joy. "Their sun shall no more go down — for the Lord shall be their everlasting light. The city had no need of the sun, neither of the moon, to shine in it, for the glory of the Lord did lighten it, and the Lamb is the light thereof."†

19. *The way of the wicked is as darkness ; they know not at what they stumble.*

The contrast is more clearly repeated.‡ Each has his own way. *The path of the just* is glowing light and joy. *The way of the wicked is darkness ;* without direction, comfort, safety, or peace, till "his feet at last stumble on the dark mountains ; " till he falls into " the blackness of darkness for ever." (Jer. xiii. 16. Jude, 13. Comp. Job, xviii. 5, 6, 18.) His *way* is not only dark, but *as darkness,* a compound of ignorance, error, sin, and misery. The love of sin " rebels against the light." (Job, xxiv. 13. John, iii. 19. Comp. Isa. v. 20.) The *darkness* is wilful, and therefore accountable. There is no *stumbling in the path of the just.* So far as he is upright, the Lord keeps him. (Verse 12 ; iii. 23. Ps. xci. 11, 12.) *The wicked* go on, " groping on as if they had no eyes " (Isa. lix. 10) ; hurrying on blindly into misery, that they can neither foresee nor avoid. (Job, v. 14 ; xii. 25. Jer. xxiii. 12. Zeph. i. 17.) *They know not at what they stumble.* Oh ! if they did, would they not startle, and shrink back ? For *they stumble* on the very foundation of the Gospel ! making the rock of salvation a rock of offence. (Rom. ix. 32, 33. 1 Pet. ii. 8.) Would they but listen to the merciful warning

---

* Reformers' Notes. Comp. Diodati *in loco.*

† Isa. lx. 20. Rev. xxi. 23. The LXX. version is very beautiful — 'The ways of the righteous shine like the light ; they go on shining, until the day be perfected.' Dr. Watts' Hymn on the Summer Evening — written for the infant mind, but glowing to the finest taste — furnishes a most exquisite exposition of this verse, —

' How fine has the day been ; how bright was the sun,' &c.

‡ See the same contrast drawn by our Lord, Matt. vi 22, 23. — Schultens considers the original to express *increasing darkness,* answering to the *increasing light* of the opposite path. Comment. in Prov. 4to. 1748. Comp. Job, xv. 23.

of their Lord — "Yet a little time the light is with you : walk while ye have the light, lest darkness come upon you ; *for he that walketh in darkness knoweth not whither he goeth.*" (John, xii. 35, 36.)

20. *My son, attend to my words; incline thine ear unto my sayings.*
21. *Let them not depart from thine eyes: keep them in the midst of thine heart.* 22. *For they are life unto those that find them, and health to all their flesh.*

These repeated injunctions (Chap. iii. 1; v. 1; vi. 20, 21; xxii. 17) are an admirable pattern to the Christian Parent 'or Minister. The desire of wisdom, the first step in the path, is encouraged. The means of obtaining, and the privilege when obtained, are pointed out. Eye, then, the treasure of wisdom habitually. A neglected Bible is the melancholy proof of a heart " alienated from God." For how can we have a spark of love to him, if that Book, which is the full manifestation of his glory, be despised ? And yet a superficial acquaintance with it is of no avail. If our ears were bored to the doors of the sanctuary ; *if the words never departed from our eyes ;* yet, except they were *kept in the heart,* our religion would be a notion, not a principle ; speculative, not practical ; conviction, not love. Nor even here must they possess the mere threshold. Let the word be *kept in the midst of the heart.* Here only can it be operative (Chap. xxiii. 26. Ps. xl. 8 ; cxix. 11) ; " for out of the heart are the issues of life." (Verse 23.) Here it becomes lively and substantial truth. Here, then, let a home be made for it,° a consecrated sanctuary in the most honoured chambers *of the heart.* This inhabitation of the word is a covenant promise — the test of our interest in the Lord. (Jer. xxxi. 33.)

This *keeping of the word* will be *life to those that find it.* (Verses 4, 10, 13 ; iii. 18.) 'Some medicines are good for one part of the body ; some for another. This is good for all the body, and all the soul.† Vigorous and *healthy* (Chap. iii. 8) shall we be, in feeding upon this heavenly manna. We shall not then bear our religion as our cross — as a cumbrous appendage. We shall not drag on in Christian duties as a chain. Godliness will be to us an element of joy. Its functions will be free and lively. The spirit will be a vital glow. The mind will be enriched with Divine wisdom. The heart will be established with gospel grace.

23. *Keep thy heart with all diligence* (above all keeping, marg.) ; *for out of it are the issues of life.* 24. *Put away from thee a froward mouth, and perverse lips put far from thee.* 25. *Let thine eyes look right on, and let thine eyelids look straight before thee.* 26. *Ponder the path of thy feet, and let all thy ways be established* (all thy ways shall be

° Ενοικείτω εν ὑμῖν. Col. iii. 16.   † Cartwright.

ordered aright, marg.) **27.** *Turn not to the right hand nor to the left: remove thy foot from evil.*

Invaluable are these rules as our safeguard. Assaulted as we are at every point, every inlet of sin must be strongly guarded — *the heart — the mouth — the eye — the feet.*

First — *the heart* — the citadel of man[*] — the seat of his dearest treasure. It is fearful to think of its many watchful and subtle assailants. Let it be closely garrisoned. Let the sentinel be never sleeping on his post. " Take heed to thy way, and *keep thy soul diligently.*" (Deut. iv. 9.)

But *the heart* must be known in order to be effectually *kept.* Nothing is more difficult, while nothing is more necessary. If we know not our hearts, we know nothing to any purpose. Whatever else we know, to neglect this knowledge is to be a fool at the best. If *we* know not our weak points, Satan knows them well — " the sins that most easily beset us."

Then when I know my heart, and feel it to be so dangerous, and in such dangers, the question forces itself upon me — ' Can I *keep my heart?*' Certainly not. But, though it be God's work, it is man's agency. Our efforts are his instrumentality. He implants an active principle, and sustains the unceasing exercise. (Phil. ii. 12, 13. Jude, 24 with 21.) Conscious faith " commits the *keeping of the heart* to our faithful Creator." (1 Pet. iv. 19. Ps. xxv. 20.) This done — in his strength and guidance diligently improve all the means of preservation. Watch unto prayer. Cherish an humble dependent spirit. Live in the atmosphere of the word of God. Resist the admittance of an evil world, even in its most plausible forms. (Judges, viii. 22, 23. 2 Kings, v. 5, 16.) Here lies the conflict to the end. ' The greatest difficulty in conversion is to win the heart to God, and after conversion to keep it with him.'[†] ' What is there ' — asks Mede — ' that will not entice and allure so fickle a thing as the heart from God?'[‡] *Above all keeping* — exhorts the wise man — *keep thine heart.* Here Satan keeps — here therefore must we keep — special watch. If the citadel be taken, the whole town must surrender. If the heart be seized, the whole man — the affections, desires, motives, pursuits — all will be yielded up. The heart is the vital part of the body. A wound here is instant death. Thus — spiritually as well as naturally — *out of the heart are the issues of life.* It is the great vital spring of the soul, the fountain of actions, the centre and the seat of principle,[§] both of sin and of holiness. (Matt. xii. 34, 35.) The natural heart is a fountain of poison. (Ib. xv. 19.) The purified heart is " a well of living water." (John, iv. 14. Compare chap. xiv. 14.) As is the fountain, so must be

---

[*] Schultens.   [†] FLAVEL's *Saint Indeed* — a searching and valuable Treatise.
[‡] See his valuable sermon on this text.   [§] Schultens.

the streams.   As is the heart, so must be *the mouth, the eyes, the feet.*
Therefore, *above all keeping, keep thine heart.*   Guard the fountain, lest
the waters be poisoned. (Comp. Gen. xxvi. 18–21.)   Many have been
the bitter moments, from the neglect of this guard.   All keeping is
vain, if the *heart be not kept.*

But with this *keeping,* let us not forget to guard the outlets of sin !
(Chap. xiii. 3.)   What a world of evil does the heart pour out from *the
froward mouth!* (Jam. iii. 5, 6.)   Commit, therefore, both heart and
mouth to Divine discipline. (Ps. xix. 13 ; cxli. 3, 4.)   Then let prayer
and faith be the practical principles of Christian watchfulness.   Not
only shun, but *put away* — yea — *far from thee* — *the perverse lips.*
Their evil — be it remembered — extends beyond ourselves.   Even
should the peace-speaking blood speak peace to ourselves, still will
remain the painful sense of injury to our fellow-creatures, perhaps
without remedy.

Next to the heart and mouth — *keep thine eyes* — "the light of the
body" (Matt. vi. 22), the directive faculty of the soul.   Yet too often
are they a most dangerous inlet to sin. (Gen. iii. 6 ; vi. 2 ; xxxix. 7.
Matt. v. 28. 2 Pet. ii. 14.)   Therefore, like Job, "make a covenant with
them." (Job, xxxi. 1.)   Place them under heavenly restraint. (Ps.
cxix. 37.)   *Let them look right on,* 'like one ploughing, who must not
look back.'°   Look *straight before us.*   Had Eve done so, she would
have looked on the command of her God, not on the forbidden tree.
(Gen. iii. 3–6.)   Had Lot's wife looked *straight before,* instead of
‚'behind her," she would, like her husband, have been a monument of
mercy. (Gen. xix. 17, 26.)   Achan was ruined by neglecting this rule
of wisdom. (Josh. vii. 21.)   David's example calls the holiest of us to
godly jealousy.†   In asking the way to Zion, be sure that your "*faces
are thitherward.*" (Jer. i. 5.)   The pleasure of sin, and the seductions of
a tempting world, do not lie in the road.   They would not therefore
meet the *eye looking right on* — *straight before us.*   They belong to the
bye-paths on the right hand and on the left, or to some backward track.
It is only, therefore, when the Christian lingers, turns aside, or turns
back, that they come in sight.   Take the racer's motto —"This one
thing I do."   Eye the mark, and press to it. (Philip. iii. 12–14.)
Onwards — upwards — heavenwards.

Lastly, *keep your feet.*   Oh ! has not experience, no less than Scripture, shown your need of a circumspect walk ? (Eph. v. 15.)   Snares
are laid out for every path, yea for every step in your path ; for your
meat, your drink, your calling — perhaps more than all — for the
service of God.   What deep *pondering* should there be in a path so
beset with danger !   Every step should be carefully weighed. (Gen.
xxiv. 5. Ps. xxxix. 1. Dan. i. 8 ; vi. 3, 4.)   Joseph *pondered,* and thereby

---

° Cartwright.   Comp. Luke, ix. 62.   † 2 Sam. xi. 2.   Mede, ut supra.

established his way. (Gen. xxxix. 9, 10. Comp. verses 14, 15.) Peter, neglecting to *ponder*, was fearfully sifted. (Matt. xxvi. 58, 69–75.) David also, looking at the trial of the path, instead of *pondering* its direction, brought shame upon himself (1 Sam. xxvii.–xxix.) ; like the trouble, which Christian made for himself in the smooth exchange of Bye-path meadow for the rough and strait road. 'The habit of calm and serious thinking makes the real difference between one man and another.'[*]

Here, then, is the voice of wisdom. Beware of mistaking presumption for faith, temptations for Providential appointments. Never forsake a plain for a doubtful command. (1 Kings, xiii. 18–22.) Estimate every step by its conformity to the known will of God. Dare not to advance one step without God. (Josh. ix. 14.) *In his path* you may "tread upon the lion and adder" without hurt. (Ps. xci. 11–13.) But who shall venture into a path of his own choosing, without a wound ? See that "your feet are straight," like those of the Cherubim.[†] "The pleasures of sin" lie *on the right hand and on the left.* *The eyes* therefore, *looking right on,* escape the sight. *The pondering foot is established* in steady perseverance ; and, by marking small deviations (See Ecclus. xix. 1), and never turning out of the straight path to avoid a cross, *is removed from evil.*

May we all have grace and wisdom to ponder these sound practical rules ! The man of God must only have one standard. (Isa. viii. 20.) He must "know no man after the flesh." (2 Cor. v. 16.) He must often put aside the Church, no less than the world, that he may listen more closely to the command— *Walk before me.* (Gen. xvii. 1.) He must discern and crush the first motions of corruption ; guarding every avenue of sin — the senses — the memory — the imagination — the touch — the taste. He must walk by the straight rule of the Gospel ; else will he not only bring discomfort upon himself, but stumbling to the Church. (Gal. ii. 11–14.) A single eye, steadily fixed upon the One Object, will make the path luminous. (Matt. vi. 22.) *Straightforward* progress will insure prosperity. (Deut. xvii. 20. Josh. i. 7, 8.) Keeping the middle path, and daily lifting up the voice for restraint and guidance. (Ps. cxix. 37 ; cxliii. 8–10.)

"Thine ears shall hear the word behind thee, saying, This is the way : walk ye in it, when ye turn to the right hand, and when ye turn to the left."[‡]

[*] Dr. Abercrombie.

[†] Ezek. i. 7–9. Comp. Heb. xii. 13. Nearly the LXX. translation of the last clause of verse 26.

[‡] Isa. xxx. 21. Comp. Deut. ii. 27 ; v. 32. The LXX. and Vulgate add here — 'For God knows the ways on the right hand. But those on the left are crooked. But he shall make straight thy paths, and advance thy goings in peace.' Geier remarks — 'We have no ear for these words, as not belonging to the holy fountain. We leave them to the Papists.' Cartwright's exposition of this middle path is valuable. 'It is as if the royal way was

CHAPTER V.

1. *My son, attend unto my wisdom, and bow thine ear to my understanding :* 2. *That thou mayest regard discretion, and that thy lips may keep knowledge.* 3. *For the lips of a strange woman drop as an honey- comb, and her mouth is smoother than oil : 4. But her end is bitter as wormwood, sharp as a two-edged sword. 5. Her feet go down to death : her steps take hold on hell. 6. Lest thou shouldest ponder the path of life, her ways are moveable, that thou canst not know them. 7. Hear me now, therefore, O ye children, and depart not from the words of my mouth. 8. Remove thy way from her, and come not near the door of her house : 9. Lest thou give thine honour unto others, and thy years unto the cruel : 10. Lest strangers be filled with thy wealth, and thy labours be in the house of a stranger ; 11. And thou mourn at the last, when thy flesh and thy body are consumed, 12. And say, How have I hated instruction, and my heart despised reproof ; 13. And have not obeyed the voice of my teachers, nor inclined mine ear to them that instructed me ! 14. I was almost in all evil in the midst of the con- gregation and assembly.*

PONDER this chapter—ye that know not the poison and corruption of fleshly lusts. Perhaps painful experience (1 Kings, xi. 1–8. Eccles. vii. 26) had given the wise man *wisdom and understanding.* Therefore *at- tend to it* with fear and trembling. Man's own strength, the restraint of education or self-discipline, is powerless, as the green withs to bind the giant. (Judg. xvi. 9.) Engrafted wisdom is the only effectual safe- guard. This heavenly influence teaches us, both to *regard discretion* for the covering of our souls, and *to keep knowledge* for the warning of our fellow-sinners. (Chap. ii. 10, 11, 16 ; vi. 20, 24 ; vii. 1–5. Ps. xvii. 4 ; cxix. 9, 11.)

The extreme plausibility of the temptation calls our *attention.* The deluded victim only tastes, or expects to taste, *the honeycomb :* only hears the *wily smoothness* of the charmer's voice. (Chap. ii. 16 ; vi. 24 ; vii. 21.) But never is the beginning so sweet as the end is *bitter.* God shows *the wormwood — the two-edged sword* (Comp. Ps. lv. 21)— her path of death — every step *taking hold of hell,* as if invading it with a high hand ; grasping it as her home. One feature of the tempter's wiliness is most remarkable.° She winds herself in a thousand *moveable ways,* to meet the varying humours and circumstances (Chap. vii. 21); she works upon every weakness ; seizes every unguarded moment—

hemmed in by the sea, and a fall over either side were danger of drowning. Some are too greedy ; others too ascetic. Some are too bold ; others too diffident. Some neglect the Mediator ; others seek new Mediators. Some flee the cross ; others make one. Some tamper with Popery ; others, from the dread of it, hazard the loss of valuable truth.'
° Schultens *in loco.* Chap. ii. 18 ; vii. 17 ; ix. 18. 1 Cor. vi. 9, 10. Rev. xxi. 8.

all with one deeply-hidden object — *lest thou shouldest ponder the path of life.* The checks of conscience must be diverted. No time must be given for reflection. The intrusion of one serious thought might break the spell, and open the way of escape. (See Ps. cxix. 59. Ezek. xviii. 28. Luke, xv. 17.)

Can we wonder then at parental earnestness, forcing back *the children* playing on the brink of a precipice? *Hear now, O ye children!* We mean no austere restraint upon youthful pleasures. Only avoid the tempter's touch, her word, even her look. *Remove thy way far from her.* Not only go not in to her ; but — such is the contagion — *come not near the door.* (Comp. ch. iv. 14, 15 ; vi. 27, 28.) To thrust ourselves into temptation, is to throw ourselves out of God's protection. The snare as it approaches becomes more enticing. The voice of wisdom therefore is — " *Flee youthful lusts.*"

The loss of *honour* (Chap. vi. 32. 33. Gen. xxxviii. 23–26), taking the crown from the victim's head (2 Sam. xii. 11 ; xv. 30. Neh. xiii. 26); *years given to the cruel* mockers of his misery (Chap. vi. 26 ; xxxi. 3. Judg. xvi. 18–21) ; the waste of the family wealth (Chap. vi. 26, 35 ; xxix. 3. Job, xxxi. 12. Hos. vii. 9. Luke, xv. 13, 30. Comp. Ecclus. v. 6) ; servitude *in a stranger's house* (Luke, xv. 15, 16) : *consumption,* slowly bringing *the body* to the grave (1 Cor. vi. 18) — such is the bitter fruit of the neglected warning. Add to this the voice of conscience *at the last,* telling of slighted privileges, stifled convictions, abused knowledge. And will not this be the sting of thousands instructed in our schools, or the children of godly parents, now *despising the reproofs* of God, *and the voice of their teachers;* proclaiming their shame openly ; perhaps making Christian *assemblies* the scenes *of almost all evil?* (Num. xxv. 6, 7. Ezek. viii. 5–16.)

Such is the picture of sin. Its " pleasure is but for a season ;" " its wages death eternal." (Heb. xi. 25. Rom. vi. 23.) Every sin unrepented here will bring its perpetual torment in eternity. Impenitence does not put away its sorrow. It only delays it to *mourn at the last,* when mercy shall have fled away for ever (Chap. i. 24–31), and nothing will remain, but the piercing cry of the accusing conscience — " Son ! remember." (Luke, xvi. 25.) There are no infidels in eternity, and but few on a death-bed. Sinner ! *the path of life* is now open to thee. *Ponder* it anxiously, prayerfully. The light of the word, and the teaching of the Spirit, guide thee to it.

15. *Drink waters out of thine own cistern, and running waters out of thine own well.* 16. *Let thy fountains be dispersed abroad, and rivers of waters in the streets.* 17. *Let them be only thine own, and not strangers' with thee.* 18. *Let thy fountain be blessed : and rejoice with the wife of thy youth.* 19. *Let her be as the loving hind and pleasant roe ; let*

*her breasts satisfy thee at all times ; and be thou ravished always with
her love.*

Desire after forbidden enjoyments naturally springs from dissatisfac-
tion with the blessings in possession.   Where contentment is not found
at home — *drinking out of our own cistern*— it will be sought for, however vainly, abroad.   Conjugal love is chief among the earthly goods
in mercy granted by God to his fallen and rebellious creature.   Enjoy
then with thankfulness thine own, and desire not thy neighbour's *well*.
(Exod. xx. 17. 2 Sam. xi. 2, 3.)   If a happy issue is given (Ps. cxxvii.
3–5 ; cxxviii.), let it be as *fountains* (Comp. Num. xxiv. 7 ; Deut. xxxiii.
28 ; Ps. lxviii. 26 ; Isa. xlviii. 1) *dispersed abroad*, to fertilize with
godly influence the way through which their course may be directed.
(Comp. Zech. viii. 5.)   *Rejoice with the wife of thy youth.* (Deut. xxiv. 5.
Eccles. ix. 9.)   Regard her as the special gift of thy Father's hand.
(Chap. xix. 14.) Cherish her with gentleness and purity (Gen. xxiv. 67),
as the loving hind and pleasant roe.†   Whatsoever interrupts the strictest
harmony in this delicate relationship, opens the door to imminent
temptation.   Tender, well-regulated, domestic affection is the best
defence against the vagrant desires of unlawful passion.   Yea — it is
consecrated by the Word of God itself to the high purpose of shadowing
out " the great mystery — loving and cherishing our own flesh, even as
the Lord the Church." (Eph. v. 25, 29.)

20. *And why wilt thou, my son, be ravished with a strange woman, and
embrace the bosom of a stranger?   21. For the ways of man are
before the eyes of the Lord, and he pondereth all his goings.   22. His
own iniquities shall take the wicked himself, and he shall be holden with
the cords of his sins.   23. He shall die without instruction; and in the
greatness of his folly he shall go astray.*

With such a view as we have had of the deadly enticement of sin
on the one hand (Verses 9–11), and the calm happiness provided on the
other by the ordinance of God (Verses 15–19), surely none but the
infatuated would leave the wholesome fountain for the poisoned and
forbidden spring.   If he were not stupified, would he slight the
" honourable " state of marriage (Heb. xiii. 4), to *embrace the bosom of a
stranger*, 'loveless, joyless, unendeared?'   Would not the thought, that

---

* The beauty of the figure is illustrated from the circumstance, that the houses of the
East appear each to have had their own cistern. 2 Kings, xviii. 31.

† Comp. 2 Sam. xii. 3. The *hind and the roe* were objects of special delight (Cant. ii.
17 ; iii. 5) and endearment — a picture of the lively delight, which the wife naturally
engages ; relaxing in her society from severer duties, and taking the liveliest pleasure in
her company. As Bishop Davenant beautifully observes — 'Abroad the man may consider
himself as tossing in the waves ; but at home with his wife, in repose, as in a desired
haven.'—On Col. iii. 19.

the ways of man are before the Lord, arrest him in his course ? ° But no.
Practical atheism is the root of human depravity. (Ps. xiv. 1–3.)   The
eye of man, even of a child, is a check upon him (Job, xxiv. 15. Isa.
xxix. 15) ; but the thought of an all-seeing God, even if it enters his
mind (Ps. x. 4), inspires no alarm, conviction, or restraint.   Oh ! if
men would but read — would but *believe* — their Bibles, how would this
solemn truth — *he pondereth all his goings* — flash upon their consciences !
Not only does he see and mark them as the Omniscient God (Job, xxxi.
4. Ps. cxxxix. 1–4) ; but *he ponders them* as the just Judge. (Chap.
xvi. 2. 1 Sam. ii. 3. Dan. v. 27.)   Not one is hidden from his piercing
eye. (Heb. iv. 13.)   " He will bring every secret thing to judgment."
(Eccles. xii. 14.)   He " will be a swift witness against the adulterers.
No unclean person shall enter into his kingdom." (Mal. iii. 2. Eph. v. 5.)

But if no regard to reason, or to the all-seeing Eye, will restrain the
sinner, let him think of the trouble that he is bringing upon himself.
God needs no chains or prison to bring him under his hand.   Wherever he goes, *his sins* go with him, as *cords to hold him* for judgment.
(Chap. xi. 3, 5, 6 ; xxix. 6. 1 Sam. xxviii. 5–10.)   Does he think that he
can give them up when he pleases ?   Repetition forms the habit.   The
habit becomes a ruling principle.   ' Every lust deals with him, as
Delilah with 'Samson — not only robs him of his strength, but leaves
him fast bound.' †   Shutting his eyes against the light, *he dies without
instruction* (Verse 12. Chap. i. 29 ; x. 21. Job, iv. 21 ; xxxvi. 12. Hos.
iv. 14, 17) — *The greatness of his folly leads him astray* — to perdition.
(2 Pet. ii. 14, 15.)

But is there no remedy for this deadly curse ?   Thanks be to God !
cleansing is provided for the impure (Zech. xiii. 1. 1 Cor. vi. 11) ;
" deliverance is proclaimed to the captive." (Isa. lxi. 1.)   Blessed
Saviour ! cleanse the leper in thy precious fountain.   Perform thy
mighty commission.   Set the captive free.

CHAPTER VI.

1. *My son, if thou be surety for thy friend, if thou hast stricken thy hand
with a stranger,* 2. *Thou art snared with the words of thy mouth,
thou art taken with the words of thy mouth.*   3. *Do this now, my son,
and deliver thyself, when thou art come into the hand of thy friend: go,*

---

* Job, xxxiv. 21, 22. Ps. xciv. 6–9. Jer. xiii. 25–27 ; xvi. 17 ; xxix. 23. Hos. vii. 2   See
some striking thoughts in MEDE's *Sermon on* iv. 23.

† Archbishop Tillotson quoted in NICHOLL's *Commentary.* Judg. xvi. 19–21.   'Thus I,'
—said Augustine—adverting to this hateful sin —' delighted with the disease of the flesh,
and with the deadly sweetness of it, drew my shackles along with me, much afraid to have
them knocked off; and, as if my wound had been too hard rubbed by it, I put back my
friends' good persuasions, as it were the hand of one that would unchain me.'— *Confess.*
b. vi. c. 12. Comp. chap. xxiii. 29–35.

humble thyself, and make sure (so shalt thou prevail with, marg.)
*thy friend.   4. Give not sleep to thine eyes, nor slumber to thine eye-
lids.   5. Deliver thyself as a roe from the hand of the hunter, and as a
bird from the hand of the fowler.*

THE *son* has just been warned against the deadly wound of a stranger.
He is now cautioned against a hurt from an imprudent friend. So graciously has our God made his book, not only our guide to heaven, but
the directory of our common life. We must, however, often take its wise
rules with some restriction. We are here earnestly warned against
suretyship.   Yet in some cases it is plainly allowed and approved.°
" A man that hath friends must show himself friendly." (Chap. xviii. 24.)
And the passing of our word, or giving a bond, may be an act of prudent friendship, and of solid and permanent advantage.   The caution
is evidently directed against rash engagements (Comp. also chap. xi. 15 ;
xvii. 18 ; xx. 16 ; xxii. 26, 27), to which the young and inexperienced
are especially exposed ; *striking with hands* (the usual mode of plighting
faith) (Chap. xvii. 18 ; xxii. 26. Job, xvii. 3), in an unguarded moment.
Often may they be *snared* and *taken by the words of their mouth,* by
entering into virtual promises, without knowing how far they were
pledged, or what might be the issue.   Christian prudence will keep us
clear from such engagements, which bring distress upon our families,
dishonour upon our name, and reproach upon our religion. (Comp.
Ecclus. viii. 13.)   While the " good man showeth favour, and lendeth,
he must guide his affairs with discretion ;" † however grating it may
be to incur the suspicion of unkindness. If, however, by any inconsiderate bond, thou hast *come into the hand of thy friend;* the instant
duty is, to *humble thyself for thy imprudence, and make sure thy friend,*
if *thou canst prevail with* him to answer for himself; and give thyself
no rest, till, *like as the roe and the bird,* thou be disentangled from the
snare.

Our God, while he warns us against *suretyship,* has taken it upon
himself.   Praised be his name ! He has given his word, his bond,
yea — his blood — for sinners — a security, that no powers of hell can
shake.

6. *Go to the ant, thou sluggard ; consider her ways, and be wise : 7. Which
having no guide, overseer, or ruler, 8. Provideth her meat in the
summer, and gathereth her food in the harvest. 9. How long wilt thou
sleep, O sluggard ? when wilt thou arise out of thy sleep ? 10. Yet a little*

---

* Reuben and Judah for Benjamin. Gen. xlii. 37; xliii. 9 ; xliv. 32, 33. Paul for
Onesimus. Philem. 18, 19.
† Ps. cxii. 5. P. Henry always cautioned sureties not to be bound for any more than
they knew themselves able to pay, nor for more than they would be willing to pay, if the
principal failed. — *Life,* chap. v.

more sleep, a little more slumber, a little folding of the hands to sleep:
11. *So shall thy poverty come as one that travelleth, and thy want as an armed man.*

' It is à shame '—said the heathen philosopher—' not to learn morals from the small animals.'[*] Yet what a proof is it of the degradation of the fall, that " man, created in the image of God," and made wiser than the creation (Gen. i. 26. Job, xxxv. 11), should be sent, as here, to this insignificant school for instruction! *The ant, having no guide* to direct her work, no *overseer* to inspect her, *or ruler* to call her to account (Comp. chap. xxx. 27, and contrast Exod. v. 13, 14; 1 Kings, v. 16); yet *gathereth* with diligent foresight the *summer and harvest* store for her winter need.[†] Let *the sluggard consider her ways, and be wise.* He sleeps over his work, and, if for a moment half-startled by some rousing call, still pleads for *a little more sleep, and folds his hands to sleep.* Present ease is all he calculates on, all he provides for. The future he carefully keeps out of sight, to be provided for, like the present, when it comes. Thus life runs to waste. *Poverty comes* step by step *as one that travelleth, and, like an armed man,* with irresistible violence. (Chap. x. 4; xiii. 4; xix. 15, 24; xx. 4; xxi. 25; xxiv. 33, 34.)

Perhaps he perverts his Master's word to excuse his sloth. But, if we are to " take no *anxious* thought for the morrow " (his true meaning),[‡] are we to take none at all? Care is a duty, a parental obligation (2 Cor. xii. 14. Comp. Gen. xxx. 30; xli. 33), and, therefore, a component part of godliness.[§] Carefulness is a sin (Luke, x. 41. 1 Cor. vii. 32), a needless burden to ourselves, an unworthy distrust of God. (Matt. vi. 25–33.) The diligent use of providential means honours God. (Chap. x. 5; xxiv. 27.)

But much more loudly would we call to the spiritual *sluggard.* Thou that art sleeping away the opportunities of grace; not " striving to enter in at the strait gate " (Luke, xiii. 24); taking thy salvation for granted; hoping that thou shalt " reap that which thou hast not sown, and gather where thou hast not strawed " (Matt. xxv. 26)—*Go to the ant, thou sluggard; consider her ways, and be wise.* Improve, after this pattern, *the summer and harvest* season—the time of youth, the present,

---

[*] Pudeat ab exiguis animalibus non trahere mores.—SENECA, *De Clementiâ.* Lib. i.

[†] Chap. x. 5; xxx. 25. Horace's miser quotes this example as an excuse for hoarding. But—as the poet replies—it was to use the hoard in the winter—prudent care, not covetousness. *Sat* i. 32. See also Virgil's exquisite picture, *Æn.* iv. 402, &c. The hoarding spirit of the ants, though attested by numerous writers and naturalists, does not characterise those known to us; though the habits of the species in a warmer climate would probably widely differ from our own. Some, however, have thought, that Solomon only refers to their wisdom and prudence in preparing suitable food in summer and harvest, when it is most plentiful.—See KIRBY and SPENCE's *Entomology,* ii. 46.

[‡] Μεριμνάω. Matt. vi. 34.—*Solicite et anxie cogito;* at plus est solicitum esse, quam cogitare, as Erasmus notices, and that of Tully confirms,—Solicitudo est ægritudo cum cogitatione. 'The root of the word expresses the dividing of the mind into divers thoughts.' —LEIGH's *Critica Sacra.* Comp. Philip. iv. 6.

[§] 1 Tim. v. 8. Our Lord had a bag for the provision of his family. John, xiii. 29.

perhaps the only, moment. *The ant hath no guide.* How many guides
have you—conscience—the Bible—ministers! (Job, xxxii. 8. Ps.
cxix. 105. Mal. ii. 7.) *She has no overseer.* You are living before Him,
whose "eyes are as a flame of fire." (Chap. xv. 3. Rev. i. 14; ii. 18.)
She has no ruler calling her to account. "Every one of us must give
account of himself unto God." (Rom. xiv. 12.) *How long then wilt thou
sleep, O sluggard?*—is the solemn remonstrance of thy God. (Comp.
chap. i. 22; 1 Kings, xviii. 21.) Thy sleep is not like that of the body,
refreshing at the dawn of day; but it is that of the poisoned draught,
heavier and heavier; the slumber of death. "Awake, thou that sleepest,
and Christ shall give thee light." (Eph. v. 14.) Slight not the call of
the present moment. The spell grows stronger, as resistance is delayed.
Every day's slumber makes it more improbable, whether thou wilt
ever awaken at all. The intended struggle of to-morrow is a delusion.
A thousand such to-morrows there may be; and yet thou mayest be
found at last perishing in thy *poverty*, and the King of terror will *come
as an armed man* to summon thee to judgment.

But how one is made to feel that from this deep slumber no voice
but Omnipotence can rouse! Enter *the sluggard's* chamber; put aside
his curtain; hang over his bed; sound a solemn cry in his ears—*How
long?* endeavour even to open his eyelids to the light of day; and yet
the spell is too strong for man. He shifts his posture, murmurs his cry
—*a little more sleep*—and slumbers again. Christians! you feel the
helplessness of your work. Then call in the power of God in your
brother's behalf—"Lighten his eyes, lest he sleep the sleep of death."
(Ps. xiii. 3.)

And then, as for thyself—grow in intense energy in thy high
calling. Remember, faith without diligence is slumbering delusion.
Faith is the practical energy of a living faith. Always, therefore, look
at sloth, not as an infirmity, but as a sin, affecting the whole man:
growing upon us with unperceived power. Allow it therefore no rest,
no time to root itself. Resist it in all its forms—bodily, mental,
spiritual: indulgence of sleep and appetite: self-pleasing in all its
subtle and plausible workings. Live by rule. Have your time strictly
arranged. Be employed in early work for God. Store the mind with
useful knowledge; ever reserving the first place for an industrious and
prayerful study of the book of God. "Mortify" this baneful lust
"through the Divine Spirit" (Rom. viii. 13); drawing all your motives
from the death (Ibid. vi. 6), the life (Mark, i. 32–35), the rules of Christ.
(Luke, ix. 23. Rom. xiii. 11–14.) Victory will soon declare for you;
and how enriching will be the spoil!

12. *A naughty person, a wicked man, walketh with a froward mouth.* 13.
*He winketh with his eyes, he speaketh with his feet, he teacheth with his
fingers.* 13. *Frowardness is in his heart; he deviseth mischief con-*

tinually; he soweth discord. 15. *Therefore shall his calamity come suddenly; suddenly shall he be broken without remedy.*

What a contrast between the inactivity of the sluggard and the unwearied diligence of *the naughty person!* This man of Belial (Heb.) — as if his *froward mouth* — itself " a world of iniquity " (Jam. iii. 6)— could not give sufficient scope for his malice, makes every member — *eyes, feet, and fingers* — vocal and significant (Isa. iii. 16), an active " instrument of unrighteousness." (Chap. x. 10. Rom. vi. 13–19.) These, however, are only the external manifestations. Deep within lies the laboratory of evil—" the chambers of imagery," teeming with " greater and yet greater abominations." (Ezek. viii. 8–15. Matt. xv. 19.) *Frowardness* is in the heart. Here is the restless *devising of mischief,†* *sowing discord,* instead of piety and love. (Chap. x. 12.) Such a pest to society brings on himself his own ruin, *suddenly and without remedy.*

The sight of this all-pervading power of sin is truly affecting. How utterly powerless is any remedy save that involved in the solemn declaration—" Ye must be born again ! " (John, iii. 7. Tit. iii. 3–5.)

16. *These six things doth the Lord hate; yea, seven are an abomination unto him :* (of his soul, marg.) 17. *A proud look, a lying tongue, and hands that shed innocent blood,* 18. *An heart that deviseth wicked imaginations, feet that be swift in running to mischief,* 19. *A false witness that speaketh lies, and he that soweth discord among brethren.*

Man conceives of God in his heart as " such a one as himself" (Ps. l. 21), looking with indifference at sin. Here therefore Solomon names *six — yea — seven* (Comp. chap. xxx. 15–18) *abominations* (most of them mentioned in the preceding list) *which the Lord hateth—a proud look,‡ a lying tongue,§* a blood-stained hand.|| And, lest we should think, that he " looketh only on the outward appearance ; " *the heart,* active in *devising wickedness,¶* is brought out ; and its ready organ, *the feet swift in running to mischief.* (Chap. i. 16. Isa. lix. 7. Rom. iii. 15.) How *hateful* also is *the false witness* (Zech. viii. 17), surely reserved by him for judgment ! (Chap. xix. 5. Zech. v. 4. Mal. iii. 5.) Let the self-willed separatist remember the double stamp (Verses 14, 19) upon him *that soweth discord among brethren.* If the heavenly " dew descends

---

* 'Frowardness,' Heb. See POOLE's *Synopsis* — not one but many ; the heart so filled with them, that the vessel cannot hold more. Gen. vi. 5. Acts, xiii. 10.

† Ps. x. 7–9 ; xxxvi. 2–4. Compare the striking figure, Hos. vii. 6. Chap. xvi. 28. Ps. lii. 2.

‡ Chap. viii. 13 ; xxx. 13. Ps xviii. 27. Isa. ii. 12. Jer. i. 31—the examples of Pharaoh — Ex. ix. 16. Haman — Esth. vii. 10. Nebuchadnezzar — Dan. iv. 28–33. Herod — Acts, xii. 21–23.

§ Chap. xii. 22. Ps. v. 6. Rev. xxi. 8. Gehazi—2 Kings, v. 25–27. Ananias and Sapphira —Acts. v. 1–10.

|| Gen. ix. 6. Cain — iv. 8–12. Manasseh — 2 Kings, xxi. 15, 16. Specially the murderers of his dear Son — Matt. xxiii. 31–38.

¶ Ahithophel — 2 Sam. xvi. 20–23 ; xvii. 23. Mic. ii. 1. 2 Pet. ii. 14.

upon the brethren that dwell together in unity" (Ps. cxxxiii.), a withering blast will fall on those, who, mistaking prejudice for principle, " cause divisions" for their own selfish ends. (Rom. xvi. 17, 18.) Fearful is the Lord's mark upon them—" sensual, having not the Spirit." [*] If we cannot attain unity of opinion—" *perfectly* joined together in the same mind, and in the same judgment ;" [†] at least let us cultivate unity of spirit—" Whereto we have already attained, let us walk by the same rule ; let us mind the same thing." (Philip. iii. 16.)

20. *My son, keep thy father's commandment, and forsake nôt the law of thy mother : 21. Bind them continually upon thine heart, and tie them about thy neck. 22. When thou gôest, it shall lead thee ; when thou sleepest, it shall keep thee : and when thou awakest, it shall talk with thee. 23. For the commandment is a lamp ; and the law is light ; and reproofs of instruction are the way of life ; 24. To keep thee from the evil woman,[‡] from the flattery of the tongue of a strange woman.*

The authority of parental instruction is again enforced. (Chap. i. 8, 9 ; iv. 1.) God never intended young people to be independent of their parents. Instruction from every quarter is valuable. But from parents—always supposing them to be godly parents—it is the ordinance of God. They will bring you God's word, not their own. Therefore *bind it continually about thine heart* (Chap. iii. 3 ; iv. 21 ; vii. 3), as thy rule ; *about thy neck* (Chap. iii. 3. Comp. Job, xxxi. 36), as thine adorning. Let the law be thy friend for all times and circumstances —a guide by day (Chap. iii. 22, 23 ; iv. 12) ; a solace by night (Chap. iii. 24. Ps. lxiii. 5), yea—a friend for thy *waking* moments. (Ps. cxxxix. 17, 18.) Take care that nothing hinders thy early converse with this faithful counsellor before the world comes in ; as the best means of keeping the world out. ' Happy is the mind to which the word is an undivided companion.'[§] 'A *lamp*, so full of *light*, in this dark world [‖] is an inestimable gift. Its *reproofs of instruction*, the discipline of our wayward will, are to us as *the way of life*. (Ps. xix. 11. 2 Tim. iii. 16, 17. Comp. Matt. vii. 13, 14.)

---

[*] Jude, 19. 1 Cor. iii. 3, 4. Let the wisdom of experience given by an accurate observer of himself and the Church, be seriously pondered—' I am much more sensible of the evil of schism, and of the separating humour, and of gathering parties, and making several sects in the Church, than I was heretofore. For the effects have shown us more of the mischiefs. I am much more sensible, how prone many young professors are to spiritual pride and self-conceitedness, and unruliness, and division, and so prove the grief of their teachers, and firebrands in the Church. I am much more sensible than heretofore of the breadth, and length, and depth of the radical, universal, odious sin of selfishness, and the excellency and necessity of self-denial, and of a public mind, and of loving our neighbour as ourselves.'— BAXTER's *Narrative of his Life and Times.*

[†] 1 Cor. i. 10—'A text'—says the godly Flavel—'to be commented upon rather by tears than by words.'—*Sermon on Text.*

[‡] Heb. Woman of wickedness—the woman full of wickedness—wholly given to it. Comp. Zech. v. 7, 8.

[§] ' Felix mens, cui verbum individuus comes.'—BERNARD, *Serm.* xxxii. *in Cant.*

[‖] Ps. cxix. 105. See Bishop Patrick's note quoted in Scott.

Specially valuable are this *lamp and light* in sensual temptation. (Chap. ii. 10, 11, 16–19 ; v. 1–8 ; vii. 1–5.) Those who choose their own light fall into a *flattering* snare. (Chap. ii. 16 ; vii. 21. The neglect of parental warning will furnish in the end bitter matter for unavailing repentance. (Chap. v. 11–13.) Oh ! let the Father's instruction be heard betimes —"Wherewithal shall a young man cleanse his way ? by taking heed thereto according to thy word." (Ps. xix. 9. Comp. v. 11 ; xvii. 4.)

25. *Lust not after her beauty in thine heart; neither let her take thee with her eyelids.* 26. *For by means of a whorish woman a man is brought to a piece of bread : and the adulteress will hunt for the precious life.* 27. *Can a man take fire in his bosom, and his clothes not be burned?* 28. *Can one go upon hot coals, and his feet not be burned?* 29. *So he that goeth in to his neighbour's wife ; whosoever toucheth her shall not be innocent.*

Solomon here gives our Lord's own rule. (Matt. v. 28. Comp. Jam. i. 14, 15 ; Job, xxxi. 1 ; Ps. cxix. 37 ; also, Ecclus. ix. 3–5.) Resist *lust* in its first rising in the heart. By vain *beauty,*° and wanton *eyes,*† many a deluded victim has been *brought to a piece of bread.*‡ Like the insatiable huntsman, who never loses sight of his prey, till he has pursued it to death ; never does the seducer cease to solicit, till she has *hunted for the precious life.* (Gen. xxxix. 14. Judg. xvi. 18–21. Comp. Ezek. xiii. 18, 20, 21.) Yet neither the present miseries, nor the certain end, of this wretched course, can draw away the foot, that has dared to tread the forbidden path. Self-confidence sees and fears no danger. ' I can look to myself; I need not go too far, and I shall get no harm.' But the temptation acts upon a congenial nature like fuel, not water, on the fire. As well might we expect to *take fire into our'bosom, and our clothes not be burned,* or to *go upon hot coals,* and *not be burned;* as to go wilfully into sin, and to escape the punishment.§ Sin and punishment are linked together by a chain of adamant. 'The fire of lust kindles the fire of hell.'‖ He cannot afterwards plead the strength of the temptation. Why did he not avoid it ? Who that knows how much tinder he carries about him, would wilfully light up the sparks ? Heedlessly to rush into temptation, is to provoke the corruption, which is too ready to stir of itself. The influence of temptation, though not

---

* Chap. xxxi. 30. Gen. vi. 2 ; xxxix. 6. 2 Sam. xi. 2. Comp. Ecclus. xxv. 21.

† Gen. xxxix. 7. 2 Kings, ix. 30. Marg. Isa. iii. 16. 2 Pet. ii. 14. Comp. *Paradise Lost,* book xi. 1, 620.

‡ Chap. v. 10; xxix. 3. 1 Sam. ii. 26, 36. Job, xxxi. 9, 12. Luke, xv. 13, 30. Comp. the difference between Solomon's chaste and unholy age. 1 Kings, x. 21, 27, with xii. 4.

§ Exod. xx. 14, 17. Lev. xx 10. 2 Sam. xii. 9. Mal. iii. 5. Even as a sin of ignorance it was liable to be visited. Gen. xii. 15–18 ; xx. 1–6 ; xxvi. 10. So strictly has the holy Lord fenced his own ordinance ! See MEDE's *Sermon on Chap.* iv. 23.

. ‖ Henry *in loco.* Comp. Job, xxxi. 12 ; Jam. i. 14, 15.

always sensible, is immediate.   The man must be in haste, who would
effectually resist it.   Beware of suspicious familiarities on the borders
of sin. (Gen. xxxix. 10. Rom. xiii. 13. 1 Thess. v. 22.)   The temptation
to criminality in this atmosphere is fearful. ('2 Sam. xi. 2–4. Comp.
Ecclus. ix. 8, 9.)   *Whosoever toucheth shall not be innocent.* (Gen. xx. 6 ;
xxxix. 9. 1 Cor. vii. 1.)

30. *Men do not despise a thief, if he steal to satisfy his soul, when he is
    hungry ; 31. But if he be found, he shall restore sevenfold ; he shall
    give all the substance of his house.   32. But whoso committeth adultery
    with a woman lacketh understanding : he that doeth it destroyeth his
    own soul.   33. A wound and dishonour shall he get ; and his reproach
    shall not be wiped away.   34. For jealousy is the rage of a man ;
    therefore he will not spare in the day of vengeance.   35. He will not
    regard* (accept the face of, marg.) *any ransom ; neither will he rest
    content, though thou givest many gifts.*

Here is no excuse or impunity for *the thief.*   The full *restitution* that
he is compelled to make °—perhaps sweeping away *all his* little *substance*—proves that no extremity can excuse " the transgression of the
law." (Comp. 1 Cor. vi. 10, with 1 John, iii. 4.)   Let him earn his bread
by honest industry.   If the fruits of industry fail, let him, trusting in
God, seek the help of his fellow-creatures.   If he have faith to trust, he
will never be forced to steal. (See Matt. vi. 25–33.)   Yet his extreme
temptation renders him an object rather of pity than of scorn — *Men do
not despise him.*

But the sin of the adulterer claims no sympathy.   His plea is not
the cry of hunger, but of lust ; not want, but wantonness ; not *the lack*
of bread, but *of understanding.* (Comp. Eccles. vii. 25, 26 ; Jer. v. 8, 21.)
He is wilfully given up to his sin.   He *destroyeth his own soul.* (Lev.
xx. 10. Chap. ii. 18, 19 ; v. 22, 23 ; vii. 22, 23. Eph. v. 5.)   *He gets a
wound*—not like the soldier or the martyr for Christ—full of honour ;
but rankling on his conscience (Ps. xxxii. 3, 4), and bringing *dishonour*
and indelible *reproach* upon his name.†   The tremendous passions of
jealousy and rage shut out all forgiveness.‡   *The face* of no one who
offered a *ransom* would be *accepted.*   No compensation (Gen. xxxix.
19, 20. Judg. xix. 29, 30), however costly, will *content.*
Such are the many sins (2 Sam. xi. 6–24), the awfully destructive

---

* Exod. xxii. 1–4.   *Seven-fold*—not literally. Four or five-fold was the extent of the
Divine requirement. Comp. Luke, xix. 8. It means full (ver. 9) and satisfactory—an
indefinite number. Comp. Gen. iv. 15, 24 ; Ps. lxxix. 12, and *alia passim.* Comp.
Job, xx. 18.
† Chap. v. 9. Gen. xxxviii. 23 ; xlix. 4. 2 Sam. iii. 18 ; xiii. 13. 1 Kings, xv. 5, with
Matt. i. 6. Neh. xiii. 26. Comp Deut. xxiii. 2.
‡ Gen. xxxiv. 7 ; xlix. 5–7. Num. v. 14. Esth. vii. 7–10. Ezek. xvi. 38. Schultens
remarks that no version fully expresses the strength of the original. *Rage,* 'Ignitio.'
In loco

miseries,* flowing from the breach of God's holy commandment. 'Oh! how great iniquity'—exclaimed the godly Augustine—'is this adultery! How great a perverseness! The soul, redeemed by the precious blood of Christ, is thus for the pleasures of an hour given to the devil; a thing much to be lamented and bewailed; when that which delighteth is soon gone, that which tormenteth remaineth without end.'†

And shall not this fearful picture of sin and its consequences (which Solomon, alas! was too well fitted to draw) teach us to avoid everything that *may be* temptation; to be sensitive to the first intimations of its becoming so; to close every avenue of sense to the entrance of this seductive poison; to shun all communications that taint the purity of taste, that familiarise the mind with impurity, that give a vivid interest to associations from which a chaste imagination recoils with disgust? Let us learn to seek Divine strength to "watch and pray" continually; and, while we "think we stand, to take heed lest we fall." (1 Cor. x. 12.)

CHAPTER VII.

1. *My son, keep my words, and lay up my commandments with thee.* 2. *Keep my commandments, and live; and my law as the apple of thine eye.* 3. *Bind them upon thy fingers, write them upon the table of thine heart.* 4. *Say unto wisdom—'Thou art my sister,' and call understanding thy kinswoman:* 5. *That they may keep thee from the strange woman, from the stranger that flattereth with her words.*

The study of wisdom in the word of God is here commended to us with affectionate earnestness, and with a beautiful variety of imagery. Let us ponder these valuable rules for practical application.

Let the whole mind and heart be occupied with it. Keep it as the daily means of *life.* (Chap. iii. 21, 22; iv. 4, 13. Isa. lv. 2, 3. Jer. xxii. 15.) Sir Matthew Hale told his children—'If I omit reading a portion of Scripture in the morning, it never goes well with me through the day.' *Lay it up* (Chap. x. 14. Deut. xi. 18. Luke, ii. 19, 51) carefully, not on our shelves, but on our hearts. Let *the whole* Word of God be our precious treasure. Receive the promises from his grace with simple affiance, and *the commandments* from his holiness with ready obedience. Stand with your eye in the land of promise; but with your feet "in the land of uprightness." (Ps. cxliii. 10.)

Maintain a jealous regard for the law. What care is necessary to *keep the apple of the eye*—that most tender part of the most tender

* The quaint lines of an old Chronicler give an awful picture—

'Corpus, opes, animum, famam, vim, lumina, scortum
Debilitat, perdit, necat, aufert, eripit, orbat.'
                                        Quoted by Trapp on verse 26.
† Lib. de Honest. Mulier. quoted by Lavater on verse 26.

member ! (Deut. xxxii. 10. Ps. xvii. 8. Zech. ii. 8.)   With the same care preserve the integrity of *the law*.   Let every part of it have its full weight.   To explain it away, or to lower its requirements, breaks down the barrier, and gives an easy entrance to temptation.   The sensual sinner is often a covert infidel.

Let it be at hand for constant use.   Bind them upon thy fingers (Chap. iii. 3. Deut. vi. 8 ; xi. 18) ; that, being always in sight, they may be always ready for the present moment.   And for their practical influence, *write them upon the table of thine heart.*   Oh! my God! this is thy Almighty work. (Isa. xxvi. 12. 2 Cor. iii. 3.)   But thou hast engaged to do it for thy people. (Jer. xxxi. 33.)   I " take hold of thy covenant." Lord! seal thy promised grace.

Let it be the object of tender affection—as our sister—our kinswoman. It is her embrace that throws the harlot's beauty into the shade.   Man must have his object of delight.   If wisdom is not loved, lust will be indulged.   The Bible therefore—not merely read, but the *cherished* object of familiar intercourse—proves a sacred exorcist to expel the power of evil. (Chap. ii. 10, 16 ; vi. 23, 24 ; xxiii. 26, 27.)

6. *For at the window of my house I looked through my casement,* 7. *And beheld among the simple ones, I discerned among the youths a young man void of understanding,* 8. *Passing through the street near her corner ; and he went the way to her house,* 9. *In the twilight, in the evening, in the black and dark night :* 10. *And, behold, there met him a woman with the attire of an harlot, and subtil of heart.* 11. *(She is loud and stubborn ; her feet abide not in her house :* 12. *Now is she without, now in the streets, and lieth in wait at every corner.)* 13. *So she caught him, and kissed him, and with an impudent face said unto him,* 14. *'I have peace-offerings with me ; this day have I paid my vows.* 15. *Therefore came I forth to meet thee, diligently to seek thy face, and I have found thee.* 16. *I have decked my bed with coverings of tapestry, with carved works, with fine linen of Egypt.* 17. *I have perfumed my bed with myrrh, aloes, and cinnamon.* 18. *Come, let us take our fill of love until the morning : let us solace ourselves with loves.* 19. *For the goodman is not at home, he is gone a long journey :* 20. *He hath taken a bag of money with him, and will come home at the day appointed.'* 21. *With her much fair speech she caused him to yield ; with the flattering of her lips she forced him.* 22. *He goeth after her straightway, as an ox goeth to the slaughter, or as a fool to the correction of the stocks :* 23. *Till a dart strike through his liver ; as a bird hasteth to the snare, and knoweth not that it is for his life.*

Solomon paints the deadly snare of *the strange woman* with a master's hand, and with exquisite fidelity of colouring.   *A young man without understanding* (Chap. i. 4, 22 ; xiii. 16) in company with *youths* as *simple* as himself, *takes in the dark of evening the way to the harlot's house.* She *meets* him. Her *attire* (Gen. xxxviii. 14, 15): her *subtilty* (Chap. xxiii. 27. Eccles. vii. 26. Judg. xvi. 4–20); her *loud and stubborn voice* (Chap. ix. 13); *her feet* at this late hour *not abiding in her house* (Comp. 1 Tim. v. 13; Tit. ii. 5); *lying in wait at every corner of the street;* ° her *impudent face* and conduct—all show the harlot's forehead. (See Gen. xxxix. 7, 12. Jer. iii. 3.) She allures her victim with the garb of sanctity. She had just been engaged in special religious duties. Now she was *come forth to seek diligently* her lover, that they might feast together upon her *peace-offerings,* † and *solace themselves with love,* with every indulgence. ' *The goodman* (perhaps the name of *husband* might have awakened conscience) *is gone a long journey till the time appointed.* Meanwhile, therefore, we may *take our fill of love* without fear of interruption.' Unarmed with principle, the weakness of resolution yields to the seduction of lust; and her unsuspecting prey rushes on to ruin.

Trace this sad end to its beginning. Was not idleness the parent of this mischief? (2 Sam. xi. 2.) The loitering evening walk; the unseasonable hour (Job, xxiv. 15. Rom. xiii. 12, 13); the vacant mind—all bringing the youth into contact with evil company (Chap. xiii. 20. 1 Cor. xv. 33)—was not this courting sin, tempting the tempter? "The house was empty," and therefore ready for his reception, and soon altogether in his possession. (Matt. xii. 44, 45.) How valuable are self-discipline, self-control, constant employment, active energy of pursuit, as preservatives under the Divine blessing from fearful danger!

See also the base varnish of religion. It is often a cover for sin! (1 Sam. ii. 22. 2 Sam. xv. 8–11. John, xviii. 28.) 'She durst not play the harlot with man till she had played the hypocrite with God, and. stopped the mouth of her conscience with *her peace-offerings.*'‡ Nay— she seems to have emboldened herself in her wickedness, as if her meeting was a happy providence, the reward of her religious services. (Verses 14, 15. 1 Sam. xxiii. 7. Zech. xi. 5.) Beware of any voice, though from the most revered quarter, that manifestly encourages forbidden indulgence.

Observe also the infatuation of the snare. 'Man cannot be ruined till he has been made confident *to the contrary.* A man must get into his victim's heart with fair speeches and promises, before he can come

---

° Chap. ix. 14, 15; xxiii. 28. Dr. Richardson mentions seeing "these wretched women in a large commercial town in Egypt, in the harlot's attire, sitting at the doors of their houses, and calling on the passengers as they went by, in the same manner as we read in the Book of Proverbs."— *Travels,* vol. i. p. 270.

† See Holden. Comp. Lev. vii. 16; xix. 6; Deut. xii. 6. Scott takes the same view— adding—'that it is no wonder, that these sacred ordinances should have given occasion to carnal indulgence, when our Christian festivals (Christmas especially) are abused for similar profanations.'

‡ Gurnal. It is a well-known fact, that the favourite mistress of Louis XIV. was so rigid in her religious duties, that her bread was weighed during Lent, lest she should transgress the austerity of fasting.

at it with a dagger.'° Thus the harlot's *flattering speech* chained the youth blindfolded for destruction. As *the ox goeth to the slaughter,* unconscious of his fate, perhaps dreaming of rich pasture : *or as a fool goeth to the stocks* (Eccles. vii. 26. Judg. xvi. 16–19), careless and un-feeling ; so does this poor deluded victim rush on with pitiable mirth or indifference, *till the dart strikes through his liver.* (Hos. iv. 11, 14.) *He hasteth as a bird to the snare* (Eccles. ix. 12), thinking only of the bait ; *and he knoweth not that it is for his life.* (Chap. ix. 18.) What will recollection bring, but the fragrance of exciting perfume (Verses 16, 17), changed into the bitterness of wormwood and gall ; the short night of pleasure succeeded by the eternal night of infernal torment ! † for a cup of pleasure drinking an ocean of wrath ! (Verse 27 ; ix. 18.)

Lastly — mark the danger of venturing into temptation. Could we expect any other results, when we *saw the youth going the way to the harlot's house?* (Chap. iv. 15 ; v. 8. Judg. xvi. 1.) He intended merely his own idle gratification ; and when he *yielded,* it was probably not without some struggle. But it is a just judgment, that those who fear not temptation should fall. ' Who would avoid danger must avoid temptation to sin. Who would avoid sin must avoid temptation to sin.'‡ The force, to which the youth's own folly subjected him, he could not plead as an excuse. When the first bounds of modesty are broken through, the door of the fancy is opened to the tempter for the kindling of lust. Thus to rush into the very jaws of ruin is to " enter into temptation" by our own will ; instead of being led or falling into it, under the providential discipline and dispensation of God. (Matt. xxvi. 41, with iv. 1. Jam. i. 2.) Self-confidence has ruined many a pro-mising profession. Tenderness of conscience, sensibility of weakness, dependence on Divine strength and promise — in this frame "he that is begotten of God keepeth himself, and that wicked one toucheth him not." (1 John, v. 18.)

24. *Hearken unto me now therefore, O ye children, and attend to the words of my mouth.* 25. *Let not thine heart decline to her ways, go not astray in her paths.* 26. *For she hath cast down many wounded : yea, many strong men have been slain by her.* 27. *Her house is the way to hell, going down to the chambers of death.*

In the hand of a licentious poet or painter, this picture might serve to contaminate the unsanctified imagination. But as it stands on the page of inspiration, it is God's solemn warning to *children,* whether in years, understanding, or experience. *Now, therefore,* that you have seen the end of sin (Verses 22, 23), *hearken unto me.* That you may *not go astray in her paths, let not thine heart decline.* (Chap. iv. 23 ; v. 8.) An impure thought, a polluted fancy, an idle book, filthy conversation,

---

* SOUTH's *Sermons,* iii. 180.
† 'Delectat in momentum ; cruciat in æternum.'—JEROME.   ‡ Geier on verse 9.

foolish company, theatres or places of vain resort—these are *her ways.*
Dread the first step, and dream not that you can stop yourself at pleasure
in her course. Familiarity with sin weakens abhorrence. Soon will
you begin to love the object of detestation. And what! should you
find too late, that you have chosen as your home her house, which is
the way to hell, and to the chambers of death?° *Many,* not of the meaner
sort, but *strong men has she cast down wounded and slain.* And a miracle
it is of Almighty power and grace, that plucks the child of God from
the brink of destruction.

Let not then the most established Christian dismiss this subject as
of no personal concern. Be it so—that "you are risen with Christ;"
that you have "set your affections on things above;" that "your life is
hid with Christ in God;" that you are looking for the glorious hope of
his "appearing." It is to you, in whom "fleshly lusts are yet warring
against the soul" (1 Pet. ii. 11), that the exhortation is given—*Mortify, therefore, your members that are upon the earth*—even the worst
members of the old man—*fornication, uncleanness, evil concupiscence.*†
And who, with the picture of *the wounded and slain* before him will
revolt?—"Is thy servant a dog, that he should do this thing?"
(2 Kings, viii. 13)—that he should need this warning? Look at the
footsteps of the *strong men* who have gone in.‡ Whom do we see come
out whole? "Behold! kings stood not before her; how then shall we
stand?" (2 Kings, x. 4.)

Nor let present steadfastness, or seclusion from temptation, blind
our eyes to the liability of yielding to the vilest indulgence. The eye
of God discerns a far deeper corruption than appears in the outer man
—such a total depravation, that even the affections, designed to be the
sources of our holiest delight, become the principle and occasion of the
most awful departures from the ways of purity and peace.

The gospel presents the only remedy. The love of Christ is the
counteracting principle to the love of lust. 'If impure love solicits,
remember the holy love of thy Saviour to thee, proved by his most
shameful death. Think of him, as looking into thy heart boiling over
with corruption, showing thee his wounds, and exciting thee to a
reciprocal love of himself.'§ The crucifixion of the flesh by a living
union with Him will "keep us from our iniquity." (Gal. v. 24, with

---

* Chap. ii. 18; ix. 18. The plural number (*the ways,* Heb.) seems to imply 'many other
ways of guilt branching out, many other paths of ruin coinciding.'—HERVEY's *Theron and
Aspasio.* Letter v. Schultens insists, that the present most wretched state, full of all
horror and execration, is included; so that the man who hath entered the seducer's house,
may be said to have entered alive into hell, and gone down to the chamber of death.—
Chap. v. 5.

† Col. iii. 1–5. Compare the exhortation to the flourishing Thessalonian Church, 1 Thess.
iv. 3–5; and to a Christian Bishop, 2 Tim. ii. 22.

‡ Samson—David—Solomon. Neh. xiii. 26.
Vestigia terrent.
Felix, quem faciunt aliena pericula cautum!

§ Geier on verse 18. Comp. 1 Cor. vi. 18, 20; 2 Cor. v. 14, 15.

Ps. xviii. 23.) " How shall we, that are dead to sin, live any longer therein?" (Rom. vi. 2, 3.) " The flesh will still lust against the Spirit." (Gal. v. 17.)   But the man, who walks with God in Gospel liberty, and Christian discipline and watchfulness, is safe. (Rom. vi. 14, with 1 Cor. ix. 27.)

But if sin be not mortified by these principles, sooner or later it will break out; if not, as here, to open disgrace; yet so as to defile the conscience, to " quench the Spirit," and by a sure, though perhaps imperceptible, course, to bring soul and body *to hell — to the chambers of eternal death.* (Rom. vi. 21. Jam. i. 14, 15.)

CHAPTER VIII.

1. *Doth not wisdom cry? and understanding put forth her voice? 2. She standeth in the top of high places, by the way in the places of the paths. 3. She crieth at the gates, at the entry of the city, at the coming in at the doors. 4. Unto you, O men, I call: and my voice is to the sons of man.*

LISTEN we now to the calls of heavenly *Wisdom* — to the voice of the Son of God.*   Careless soul! shall thy Divine call be slighted, when the allurements of sin and vanity have had power to arrest thine ear? † Can ignorance be pleaded?   *Doth not wisdom cry?* and that — not in the hour of darkness, and in the secret corners, but in the *high* places — *the paths of the city — the doors* of thy house?   Has she not followed thee to thy places of business — of diversion — of sin?   Has she *not put forth her voice* in the Bible — in the family — in the preached word? The loudness — the perseverance of the *cry* betokens earnestness in thy

---

* We assume the speaker to be personal — essential Wisdom. Apart from the general reasons before given (Notes on chap. i. 20, 21, 24), this description could not without unnatural force apply to an attribute It set out, I. *Personal existence — brought forth — brought up* — in conjunction with Deity — *by Him* (verses 24, 30.) II. *Personal properties* (1.) *set up* (anointed, Heb.) *from everlasting*, for distinct office (verse 23), (2.) *The efficient cause in the work of creation* (verses 27-30), (3.) Having *wisdom* (verse 14) which, as an attribute itself, could not be the property of an attribute; *and strength* (verse 14) an independent quality, not a property of wisdom, (4.) Personal authority (verses 15, 16), (5.) Leading into the ways of truth (verses 19, 20), (6.) Causing to inherit. (Verse 21.) III. Personal affections — hatred (verse 13), love (verse 17), joy. (Verses 30, 31.) IV. Giving personal promises. (Verse 21.) V. Commanding obedience as a matter of life and death. (Verses 32-36.) Whether Solomon fully understood his own words, may be a question. 1 Pet. i. 10, 11. But receiving the words as from God; weighing their natural force; comparing them with Scripture parallels, we doubt not that they describe — not an attribute, but a Person — Eternal — Omniscient — in the most endearing relation to man — his Creator — Mediator — Saviour.

† Chap. vii. 'Imagination cannot form to itself a more exquisite and affecting piece of scenery, than that exhibited by Solomon in the Book of Proverbs. In his seventh chapter he introduces the world, by its meretricious blandishments alluring the unwary to the chambers of destruction. In the succeeding chapter, by way of perfect contrast, appears in the beauty and majesty of holiness, the Son of the Father, the true and eternal Wisdom of God, with all the tender love and affectionate concern of a parent, inviting men to the substantial joys and enduring pleasures of immortality, in the house of salvation.'—Bishop HORNE's *Sermon on the Tree of Knowledge.*

friend, and danger in thy condition. For would she have cried so loud, or continued so long, if she had not loved thy soul; if she had not known the wrath that was hanging over thee — the hell that was before thee?

The call is unfettered; not to devils, but *to men:* not to the righteous, but *to the sons of men.* Every child, therefore, of guilty Adam has his name in the warrant. It is the proclamation of the Gospel " to every creature." (Mark, xvi. 15.) Wherever the word reaches, the offer is made. Wherever a lost sinner be found on this side of the grave, the free welcome of the Gospel meets him. If he be not saved, he is more lost than ever. His ruin lies at his own door. (Matt. xxiii. 37.)

5. *O ye simple, understand wisdom: and, ye fools, be ye of an understanding heart.* 6. *Hear; for I will speak of excellent things; and the opening of my lips shall be right things.* 7. *For my mouth shall speak truth; and wickedness is an abomination to my lips.* 8. *All the words of my mouth are in righteousness; there is nothing froward or perverse in them.* 9. *They are all plain to him that understandeth, and right to them that find knowledge.* 10. *Receive my instruction, and not* silver; and knowledge rather than choice gold.* 11. *For wisdom is better than rubies: and all the things that may be desired are not to be compared to it.*

The great Teacher calls *the simple and fools to hear.* (Chap. i. 23; ix. 4, 5.) And where 'else can they hear such *excellent things?* Worthy are they of the attention of princes † — his glorious person; his everlasting covenant; his rich and sovereign love to sinners. (Verses 12–31.) Often does the truth of God, by the tradition of men,‡ or the subtilty of the father of lies (Comp. Matt. iv. 6, 7, with Ps. xci. 11), become virtually a principle of error. (Gal. i. 7–9.) But here *all* is unchangeable *righteousness.* There is no *froward perversion.* *Every such wickedness is an abomination.* (Chap. xxx. 5. Ps. xix. 9; xxxiii. 4; cxix. 152, 160.)

But are they within the reach of the multitude? They who "lean to their own understanding " (Chap. iii. 5. 1 Cor. i. 20; iii. 18); who care more to be learned than to be holy; who value the tree of knowledge more than the tree of life; who desire " meat for their lust," rather than manna for their souls. Such, indeed, make difficulties for themselves. The " voice out of the whirlwind " rebukes them, as " darkening counsel by words without knowledge." (Job, xxxviii. 1, 2.) Scripture difficulties belong not to the Book itself, but to man's blind and

---

* Rather than silver. See next clause, and Comp. Hos. vi. 6.

† Heb. princely.

‡ It was a keen reply of one of the Martyrs, when asking of Bonner's chaplain —'Is not God's book sufficient for my salvation?'—the answer was—'Yes, it is sufficient for our salvation; but not for our instruction.' 'God send me the salvation, and you the instruction.'—Exam. of Thomas Hawkes. Foxe, vii. 100.

corrupt heart. The carnal man cannot understand it, any more than
the blind can see the noon-day light of the sun. But 'it is easy to all
that have a desire to it, and which are not blinded by the prince of this
world.'° The "babes" are taught of God. (Matt. xi. 25 ; xviii. 4.)
He not only unfolds the truth, but opens their hearts to receive it.
There will be, indeed, great depths. But they will grasp important,
saving truths. Here 'the wisest Solomon may fetch jewels for ornament, and the poorest Lazarus bread for life.'† Come then — sinner —
"sit," with one of old, "at the feet" of thy Divine Teacher. (Luke,
x. 39.) *Receive his instruction* more precious *than silver or fine gold.*
(Verse 19 ; xvi. 16. Job, xxviii. 15–19. Ps. xix. 10 ; cxix. 127.) Enrich
thyself with his satisfying and enduring treasures, *compared with which
all the things that may be desired* are lighter than vanity. (Chap. iii. 15.)
And will not the children of God daily draw more abundantly from
these treasures? Oh! let them not be, like the pomp of this world,
the object of gaze, but of active desire and increasing enjoyment.

12. *I wisdom dwell with prudence, and find out knowledge of witty in-*
ventions.

How adorable is the Being here before us! His glorious perfections, each *dwelling with* the other in such harmonious combination!
All the *witty inventions* of science are ultimately traceable to this heavenly source. (Exod. xxxi. 3–6 ; xxxv. 30–35. 1 Chron. xxviii. 19. Isa.
xxviii. 24–29.) But his great mind was soaring far beyond. The vast
discovery of man's salvation was now before his eyes (Verses 22–31) ;
found out, not by laborious investigation, but by the intuition of the
Infinite Godhead. Here is his most splendid display of *wisdom* (Eph.
iii. 10) *dwelling with prudence* — *wisdom* contriving for the highest end :
prudence directing the most effective means. The same perfect combination controls all his arrangements, both as "the Head of the
Church" (Col. i. 18), and "the Head over all things to his Church"
(Eph. i. 22), for her present good, and his eternal glory. And what
owe we individually, to "the riches of his grace, wherein," by the
removal of insuperable difficulties, and the communication of suitable
grace, "he hath abounded towards us in all *wisdom and prudence!*"
(Ib. i. 7, 8.)

Prudence is commonly thought to be only a moral quality. Here
we see it to be an attribute of Deity. The humanity of our beloved
Lord was filled with this perfection. (Isa. xi. 2.) With what Divine
acuteness of *wisdom* did he *find out the knowledge of the inventions* of his

* Reformers' Notes. Comp. chap. xiv. 6 ; xvii. 24. 'What wonder, if the unlettered
and despised Christian know more of the mysteries of Heaven than the naturalists, though
both wise and learned? Christ admits the believer into his bosom, and *He* is in the bosom
of the Father.'—LEIGHTON's *Sermon on Heavenly Wisdom.*
† Bishop REYNOLDS *on Hos.* xiv. 9.

enemies, and put them to shame! (Matt. ix. 4–8 ; xxii. 15–46.)   And
how did this combination of *prudence* restrain him from hasty confidence
(John, ii. 23, 24), remove him from premature danger (Matt. xii. 14–16.
John, vi. 15), and preserve him from giving needless offence! (Matt.
xvii. 27.)   Praised be our God for such "treasures of *wisdom*," hid in
"our glorious Head," ready for distribution for every emergency of his
people's need! (Col. i. 19 ; ii. 3.)

13. *The fear of the Lord is to hate evil : pride, and arrogancy, and the evil*
way, and the froward mouth, do I hate.

Such is the holiness of Divine *wisdom!*   She *dwells with prudence.*
But she cannot dwell with evil.   Therefore, *the fear of the Lord*, which
is her very nature, is *to hate evil*. (Chap. iii. 7 ; xvi. 6.)   Thus of *pride*
in all its branches—*arrogancy* of spirit, *the evil way and the froward*
mouth—the Wisdom of God declares without reserve—*I hate them.*
(Chap. vi. 16–19 ; xvi. 5. Ps. xlv. 7. Zech. viii. 17.)   How clearly did
he mark his *hatred* in the days of his flesh by the full exhibition of the
opposite grace!   "The Son of man came not to be ministered unto,
but *to minister.*" (Matt. xx. 28. Luke, xxii. 27.)   A proud disciple of a
lowly Saviour! how offensive is this contradiction to our Master! What
a cause of stumbling to the world!

14. *Counsel is mine, and sound wisdom ; I am understanding ; I have*
strength.

This *counsel*, as we have just hinted (See on verse 12), is not, as
with man, the fruit of deliberation, but Divine intuition.   It is not that
it flows from him ; but that he is himself the essence—the fountain-
head. (Isa. xl. 13, 14. Rom. xi. 34.)   It is not that he *hath understanding*
to order and govern the world.   But *he is understanding.*   All is in
him.   All is derivable from him. (John i. 9.)   "His understanding is
infinite ; his *strength* Almighty, everlasting." (Ps. cxlvii. 5. Isa. xl. 28 ;
xxvi. 4.)   Thus we adore him—we rest in him—as the great "Counsellor" (Isa. ix. 6) ; One with his Father in the everlasting plan of
salvation (Zech. vi. 12, 13) ; One with his Church, undertaking her
cause (Ib. iii. 1), guiding her in all her difficulties and perplexities.
(Isa. lxiii. 9–14.)   His self-existent power is ever ready to execute the
purpose of his *counsel*. (Ib. verses 1–6. Ps. lxxxix. 19. Job, ix. 4 ;
xii. 13, 16. Dan. ii. 20.)   Behold him then, surrounded with the majesty
of his mighty perfections—"Christ, the power of God, and the wisdom
of God." (1 Cor. i. 24.)   In all thy doubts and anxieties—*counsel is*
mine, and sound wisdom. (Isa. xlviii. 17.)   In all thy conflicts and
weariness—*I have strength.* (Ib. xl. 28, 29.)   See him as man filled
with these Divine perfections. (Ib. xi. 2.)   Remember—his fulness
is thy portion. (1 Cor. i. 30. Col. ii. 10.)

15. *By me kings reign, and princes decree justice.* **16.** *By me princes rule, and nobles, even all the judges of the earth.*

Another glorious contemplation of this Divine Person! He proclaims himself to be the source of power and authority, no less than of *counsel and wisdom.* "KING OF KINGS was" the mysterious name written upon his vesture. (Rev. xix. 16; i. 5; xvii. 14.) Yet his crown does not displace the regal diadem from the brow of earthly princes; nor is the sceptre to fall from their hands. These ensigns of power are to be held, but in subordination to his own. *By me kings reign;* not only by my permission, but by my appointment. They bear my name. They are stamped with my authority. (Exod. xxii. 28. Ps. lxxxii. 6. John, x. 35.) Proud anarchy disputes the prerogative, and traces the authority to the people; only that they may cast off the yoke of God, and "do that which is right in their own eyes." (Judg. xvii. 6; xix. 1. Hos. viii. 4. 2 Pet. ii. 10. Jude, 8.) Scripture polities lay down the offensive truth —"There is no power but of God; the powers that be are ordained of God. They are ministers of God," not servants of the people. (Rom. xiii. 1–6.) Government in all its administrations—kings, princes, nobles, judges—is a Divinely-consecrated ordinance.° Every kingdom is a province of the universal empire of the "King of kings." Men may mix their own pride, folly, and self-will with this appointment. But God's providential counter-working preserves the substantial blessing. Yet, if "the power be *exclusively* of God," then is *Wisdom, by whom kings reign,* the very essence and person of God. And here is our rest, our anchor in this world's agitating storm. "The government of the world is on the shoulders" of "the Head of the Church." (Isa. ix. 6.) All things— all power in heaven and in earth —is delivered unto him of his Father.† "The Lord reigneth; let the earth rejoice." (Ps. xcvii. 1.)

17. *I love them that love me; and those that seek me early shall find me.*

Now behold the grace of this Divine Person to his *loving* children. None by nature are interested in it. (Rom. viii. 7.) But his free grace first implants *love* in their hearts, and then cheers them with the assurance of his own *love.* (1 John, iv. 19. John, xiv. 21.) The first kindling of the flame is of him. We *love,* because we are drawn. (Jer. xxxi. 3.)

---

* Ps. lxxv. 7. Jer. xxvii. 5–7. Dan. ii. 37, 38; iv. 25; v. 18. Comp. John, xix. 11. It is interesting to trace this acknowledgment even in the darkness of Heathenism. Kings inherited their sceptre from Jove; Magistracy was consecrated by Augurs, the Assessors and Counsellors of Jove.

† Matt. xi. 27; xxviii. 18. Scott remarks the future tense in the original, as seeming to agree with the prediction of righteous kings and rulers in the latter times of the Church. Comp. Ps. lxxii. 1–8; Isa. xlix. 23; lx 16, 17. See the national blessing of godly rulers— 2 Chron. ix. 8. Isa. i. 26.

We *seek*, not by the impulse from within, but by the grace from above (Chap. xvi. 1. Ps. cxix. 32) ; and *seeking, we find.* (Isa. xlv. 19. Jer. xxix. 13. Matt. vii. 7, 8.)   But it must be *early seeking*—*the first desire and choice of the heart.* (Chap. xxiii. 26. Ps. lxiii. 1. Hos. v. 15. Matt. vi. 33.) It must be *early in the day* (Ps. v. 3 ; cxix. 147. Isa. xxvi. 9. Mark, i. 35), the first-fruits of our time. Consecrate the whole to him. Take care that God is the first person we speak to ; that we see his face *first* before any other ; else will our lamp be untrimmed, our soul estranged from his presence, our heart unready for his service. *Let it be the early breaking in of the day of grace* (Job, viii. 5–7. Isa. lv. 6. 2 Cor. vi. 2)— the improvement of the first—who knows that they be not the only— opportunities of salvation ? (Chap. xxvii. 1. Heb. iv. 7.)   Every present opportunity for the soul is worth worlds.   Mercy is in it—grace and glory are in it—heaven and eternity are in it.   But remember—the door of grace, that is opened to-day, may be shut to-morrow—for ever.

Again—this *early seeking.*   Oh! let it be the early spring and morning of life (1 Kings, xviii. 12. 2 Chron. xxxiv. 3.)—when the eye is full of life, and the heart of gladness.   Let it be " the kindness of youth" (Jer. ii. 2) " the first love :" before it has been devoted to the world ; before the hardening habits of sin have been formed and fixed. Is he not the greatest—the most desirable—the most satisfying good ? Therefore, let him be to us—as he deserves to be—the first of the first —the best of the best.

Children !   Here is a special encouragement for you, added to the general one.   It can never be too early for you.   Even now it is too late.   God has claimed you from the moment that you passed from unconscious infancy to the dignity of a responsible being.   The time spent, so long estranged from God, has been all too long.   Early de- votedness saves from many follies and mistakes, retracing of steps, and the after misery of being " made to possess the iniquities of our youth." (Job, xiii. 26.)   Early satisfaction—the pure fruit of *early seeking*— (for they that thus *seek shall find*) will be the joy of your whole life (Ps. xc. 14, with verses 34, 35)—the dawn of your blessed eternity. Remember—the bud and bloom of life is specially acceptable to God (Hos. xi. 1–4) ; specially honoured by him. (1 Sam. ii. 18 ; iii. 19. Ps. xcii. 12–15.)   But is it reasonable—nay—is it not a most abasing thought—to offer the flower of youth to Satan ; and, when you have well worn yourself out in his service, to reserve only the dregs and sweepings of life for your Saviour ? (Mal. i. 8.)   Every day you lose a world of happiness ; you bind a chain of sin ; you take a step to hell. Come, then, and answer the call that is drawing you to Him, who is worthy of all. (1 Sam. iii. 9. Ps. xxxii.'8. Jer. iii. 4.)   Never will you regret that you have come too soon.   But many have been the sor- rowing cries—Lord, ' I have loved thee too late !' (Matt. xxv. 6–12.

Luke, xiii. 24, 25.) Come, then, by his help, and in dependence on his grace make him your first, your present choice. Lay claim by faith to this promise to *early seekers, and you shall find.*

18. *Riches and honour are with me : yea, durable riches and righteousness.* 19. *My fruit is better than gold, yea, than fine gold ; and my revenue than choice silver.* 20. *I lead in the way of righteousness, in the midst of the paths of judgment :* 21. *That I may cause those that love me to inherit substance ; and I will fill their treasures.*

What a treasure do *early seekers find !* This fading world is too poor a portion. (Ps. xvii. 14, 15.) Theirs are *durable riches* of eternity (Matt. vi. 19, 20. Luke, x. 42. Rev. iii. 18) ; the *honour* of " reigning" as kings " in life" (Rom. v. 17 ; viii. 17. Rev. i. 6) ; *a righteousness,* in which they are accepted with God, and conformed to his image. (Rom. iii. 22 ; xiii. 14. Eph. iv. 24.) Is not this *fruit and revenue better than choice silver ?* (Verses 10, 11 ; iii. 14, 15. Eccles. vii. 12.) And then, when our way is shut up, how valuable is Wisdom's counsel ! (Chap. iii. 6 ; iv. 11, 12 ; vi. 22. Isa. xlviii. 17 ; xlix. 10) so carefully *leading in the midst of the paths;* ' at a distance from the extreme'* on either side of the narrow way. The sober-minded Christian is equally remote from formal service and enthusiastic delusion. His apprehensions of truth are alike distinguished from the dryness of system, and from loose unconnected principles. The intelligent and spiritually-minded Church-man is alike separate from exclusiveness or idolatry on the one side, and from indiscriminate Christianity on the other. He values highly his Scriptural ordinances ; yet he neither mistakes them for the substance of the gospel, nor does he substitute self-willed effervescence in their room. This is the *Via Media*—Christian unity, consistency, and fruitfulness. Here also is *substance*—things that have a being, in contrast with " things that have not" (Chap. xxiii. 5. Ps. xxxix. 6. 1 Cor. vii. 31) ; solid realities (Isa. xxix. 8, contrasted with Isa. lv. 2) ; " faith substantiating things hoped for." (Heb. xi. 1.) Sin pardoned : the Father smiling acceptance ; the Comforter witnessing our peace ; a new moulding of our mind and spirit. Here is no yawning vacuum, but a grand object to give interest to life, to fill up every vacancy in the heart—' perfect happiness.' † All that we could add from the world would only make us poorer, by diminishing that enjoyment of God, for the loss of which there is no compensation. There is one point—only one—in the universe, where we can look up, and cry with the saintly Martyn—' With thee there is no disappointment.' ‡

Now contrast the portion in this life—of the men of this world. Mark how the word of God pictures it—a fashion (1 Cor. vii. 31)—a

---

* Scott. Chap. iv. 25-27. See Bunyan's fine description of the middle path.
† Cartwright.   ‡ *Journals,* vol. ii. 130.

dream (Ps. lxxiii. 20) — a nonentity (Chap. xxiii. 5. Amos, vi. 13) — a lie. (Jonah, ii. 8.) Thus men are spread over the world, "feeding upon ashes, a deceived heart turning them aside." (Isa. xliv. 20.) The inlet of their misery is, that they walk in a vain shadow, and "therefore they are disquieted in vain." The child of God finds *substance* in "returning to his" true "rest. Now, Lord, what wait I for? my hope is in thee." (Ps. xxxix. 6, 7.)

But how does he come to his portion? Has he any part in deserving it? Far from it. Free grace, not free will, is the procuring cause. It is an *inheritance*, now indeed "obtained," while "the earnest" is in hand (Eph. i. 11); but to be fully enjoyed at the great consummation-day. Then, indeed, what here he promises will he fully make good. His joyous welcome "to them on his right hand" will indeed be *causing them that love him to inherit substance* (Heb. x. 34) — eternal, unfading. (Matt. xxv. 34.) Even now from his royal bounty does he *fill their treasures.* But what will be the burst of joy at that day — what the unbounded delight throughout eternity, when, endowing them with such a royal — yea — Divine bounty, the glorious Giver shall proclaim — *I will fill their treasures!* (1 Pet. i. 4, 5.) And the countless throng of the redeemed shall unite in the testimony — *One Christ hath abundantly filled us all!*

22. *The Lord possessed me in the beginning of his way, before his works of old. 23. I was set up from everlasting, from the beginning, or ever the earth was. 24. When there were no depths, I was brought forth: when there were no fountains abounding with water. 25. Before the mountains were settled, before the hills was I brought forth: 26. While as yet he had not made the earth, nor the fields, nor the highest part of the dust of the world. 27. When he prepared the heavens, I was there; when he set a compass upon the face of the depth: 28. When he established the clouds above: when he strengthened the fountains of the deep: 29. When he gave to the sea his decree, that the waters should not pass his commandment: when he appointed the foundations of the earth: 30. Then I was by him, as one brought up with him: and I was daily his delight, rejoicing always before him; 31. Rejoicing in the habitable part of his earth: and my delights were with the sons of men.*

It must be a perverted imagination that can suppose an attribute here. So glorious are the rays of eternal supreme Deity, distinct personality, and essential unity, that the mysterious, ever-blessed Being — "the Word, who was in the beginning with God, and was God" (John, i. 1, 2) — now undoubtedly stands before us. Curiously to pry into the mode of his subsistence, would be "intruding into those things which we have not seen." (Col. ii. 18. 1 Tim. vi. 16.) To receive his own revelation of himself is our reverential privilege.

How clear is his essential unity with the Father! The Lord possessed° *me*—present with him in the bosom of Deity. Every movement of the Divine mind was infinitely known—every purpose of Divine counsel eternally present—fully developed, *I was by Him* †—in the same essence and blessedness. (John, x. 30.) Such was "the glory which he had with the Father before the world was!" (Ib. xvii. 5.) Neither man nor angel could declare it. No created intelligence could tread one footstep in the course, that realises any conception of the mystery. The mode of his existence in the Godhead (and this is all that is revealed of this inscrutable subject) is generation—*I was brought forth*—"the only-begotten Son" ‡—a term which it is much safer to adore than to expound; expressing, as it does, what is unsearchable. 'Take care'—saith an old expositor—'that in this generation we invent nothing temporal, carnal, or human. But rather let us worship this generation, beholding it by faith; and let us take heed from searching further than Scripture doth teach us thereof. Otherwise we should deserve to be blinded and punished for our great curiosity.' §

Not less clear is his eternal existence—*in the beginning* ‖ *of the way of God*—coeval with his eternal counsels—*before his works of old* ¶—*set up or anointed* °° *from everlasting* for his covenant offices (1 Pet. i. 20); 'destined and advanced to be the Wisdom and Power of the Father, Light and Life, and All in All, both in the creation and the redemption of the world.' ††

Connected with his eternity was his agency in the work of Creation. Before the works was he brought forth. But *when* they were in operation *he was there*—and that, not, like "the sons of God," an interested

---

* LXX. and Syriac Translation—'*created*'—most unwarrantable—one of the main pillars of the Arian heresy.

† John, i. 2. Geier remarks, that out of above sixty instances, where this preposition occurs, not óne can be produced, where vicinity is not supposed between two distinct persons or substances.

‡ John, i. 18; iii. 16. Col. i. 15—'begotten before every creature.'—Bishop MIDDLETON.

§ COPE (MICHAEL), *Exposition of Proverbs.* 4to. 1580.

‖ Holden strongly advocates the Translation—supported by many Ancient Versions, and some of the best critics (see POOLE's *Synopsis*)—'the beginning of the way'—and expounds it—'That Jehovah possessed by an eternal generation Wisdom or the Son, who is the origin, or efficient cause, of all the works of God.'—Comp. Col. i. 18. Rev. iii. 14, also i. 8; xxii. 13. Geier and other accredited authorities prefer the received version upon critical grounds. Holden's remark, however, holds good on either hypothesis:—'It is scarcely possible in the whole compass of the Hebrew language to select terms more expressive of the eternity of Wisdom than those which Solomon employs from this verse to the thirtieth.'

¶ Contrast Job, xxxviii. 4, 5. Comp. verses 23-25, with Ps. xc. 2—the sublime adoration of the eternity of God. Comp. also Exod. iii. 14, with John, viii. 58. Mic. v. 2. Rev. i. 11.

** Heb. Anointing was the inaugurating ceremony in the consecration of prophets, priests, and kings—a figure of the eternal consecration of Messiah to those high offices. Comp. 1 Kings, xix. 16, with Isa. xli. 1; lxii. 1. Exod. xxix. 7, with Ps. cx. 4. 1 Sam. x. 1; xvi. 13. 2 Kings, ix. 6, with Ps. ii. 6, marg. xlv. 6, 7.

†† HENRY *in loco.* Comp. Eph. iii. 9.

spectator (Job, xxxviii. 6, 7), but an efficient cause.° The whole detail of the creative work is brought out — *the highest part* or summits *of the dust of the world*, with its deep and unsearchable *foundations*. Thus is uncreated Wisdom displayed in clear and undoubted glory—'the Divinity and eternity of Wisdom, meaning thereby the eternal Son of God, Jesus Christ our Saviour.' †

Next he describes his *unspeakable blessedness in communion with his Father. I was by him, as one brought up with him* — embosomed in him as the object of *daily delight ;* ‡ rejoicing before him as the Fountain and Centre of infinite joy. All this mutual intimate satisfaction and *delight* had respect to the *beginning of the way of God — his* eternal purpose, and "the counsel of peace, which was between them both." (Zech. vi. 13.) Here it was that the Father once and again proclaimed him to be *his delight;* "His elect, in whom his soul delighted ; his beloved Son, in whom he was well pleased" (Isa. xlii. 1. Matt. iii. 17 ; xvii. 5. Comp. Col. i. 13, Gr.) ; 'willing that by the Son we should approach to him ; in the Son we should honour and adore him ; and honour the Son as himself.' §

Yet how deeply interesting is it to see him rejoicing, not only before his Father, but in the habitable part of the earth! And what was it that here attracted his interest ? Man had been created in the image of God — free to stand or fall. This freedom was the perfection of his nature. His fall was permitted as the mysterious means of his higher elevation. His ruin was overruled for his greater security. This *habitable earth* was to be the grand theatre of the work, that should fill the whole creation with wonder and joy. (Ps. xcviii. Isa. xliv. 23.) Here "the Serpent's head was to be visibly bruised" (Gen. iii. 15. Heb. ii. 14, 15. 1 John, iii. 8), the kingdom of Satan to be destroyed, precious "spoil to be divided with the strong." (Isa. liii. 12. Luke, xi. 21, 22.) Here was the Church to be framed, as the manifestation of his glory, the mirror of all his Divine Perfections. (Eph. iii. 10, 21.)

Considering the infinite cost at which he was to accomplish this work — the wonder is — that he should have *endured* it — a greater wonder that, ere one atom of the creation was formed — ere the first blossom had been put forth in Paradise, he should have *rejoiced* in it.

But the wonder *of wonders yet remains* — that he, who was his

---

* John, i. 3. Col. i. 16. Even in the creation of man he was a co-worker, Gen. ii. 7, with i. 26.

† Reformers' Notes.

‡ Comp. John, i. 18 — *the only-begotten Son, who is in the bosom of the Father —* 'exhibiting at once,' as Dr. Jamieson admirably observes—'the idea conveyed by both the terms — *brought forth, and brought up.'— Vindication of Doctrine of Deity of Christ,* i. 224. Holden with some others prefers the rendering 'Fabricator' for *brought up.* But the scope appears to be—not the power of Messiah, but the mutual delight and communion between himself and his Father, as it were, never absent from each other.

§ Quoted by Scott.

Father's infinite delight, and infinitely delighting in him, should find *his delights* from all eternity *in the sons of men;* that he should, as it were, long to be with us; that he should solace his heart with the prospect; that he should anticipate the moment with joyous readiness (Ps. xl. 6–8. Heb. x. 7); that he should pass by the far nobler nature of angels " to take hold of man " (Heb. ii. 16, marg.), to embrace man as one with his All-perfect self!   But though he foresaw how they would despise, reject, and put him to shame; yet they were the objects of his everlasting love (Jer. xxxi. 3.), the purchase and satisfaction of the " travail of his soul " (Isa. liii. 10, 11), the eternal monuments to his praise (Ib. lv. 13). Yet for their sakes did he make humanity·a temple of the Deity, for them did he exchange the throne of glory for the accursed cross (Philip. ii. 6–8) — the worship of the Seraphim for the scorn and buffeting of men (Isa. vi. 1, 2, with Matt. xxvii. 22–31) — inexpressible joy for unknown sorrow. (John, xvii. 5, with Matt. xxvi. 38; xxvii. 46.)   Yes — thou adorable Redeemer, nothing but the strength of thine own love could have brought thee out from the bosom of ineffable delight to suffer such things for such sinners!   But this was " the joy set before thee, for " which — unfathomable love! — thou wast content "to endure the cross, despising the shame." (Heb. xii. 2.) For this love dost thou inherit thy Father's justly proportioned reward. (Philip. ii. 8–11.) On this foundation is thy people's confidence — rest — security.

32. *Now therefore hearken unto me, O ye children : for blessed are they that keep my ways.   33. Hear instruction and be wise, and refuse it not.*

Now therefore hearken.   It is no mean and undeserving person that calls.   It is none other than the Wisdom of-God; the source of all light and knowledge (Verses 12–14) ; the King of kings (Verses 15, 16) ; the loving rewarder of his children, especially of his young children (Verse 17. Comp. Heb. xi. 6); the rich portion and unfailing guide of his people: (Verses 18, 19.)   Look at him once again in his Divine glory, as " the only-begotten Son of God " (Verses 22, 24) ; the Mediator in the everlasting Councils of Redemption (Verse 23) ; the Almighty Creator of the world (Verses 27–30) ; the adorable Friend of sinners (Verse 31). How should his Divine Majesty and condescending love endear his *instruction* to us!°   Yet his promised *blessing* belongs only to practical hearing — to *those that keep his ways* (Isa. lv. 2, 3. Luke, xi. 28. John, xiv. 21–23. Jam. i. 25) with godly fear, constancy, and perseverance; keeping their eye on them, their hearts towards them, their feet in them.   Such *are* truly *blessed.* They choose rightly ; they walk surely ; they live happily ; they progress honour-

---

° See how the Father manifested the glory of his Divine Son to give constraining force to his instruction.   Matt. xvii. 1–5.

ably ; they end gloriously. Is it not therefore our *wisdom to hear instruction* with " the obedience of faith "—not doing what he commands — (in which we may sometimes do — not his will, but our own) but doing because he commands — doing his will in it — obeying as well when it crosses our nature, as when it is more congenial with it ? But for this cheerful, child-like obedience, sovereign grace must open the heart, and give the ear. (Chap. xx. 12, with Acts, xvi. 14.) The guilt of *refusing* is inexcusable — a resolved will against the most gracious call. (Acts, iii. 22, 23. Heb. ii. 1–3.)

Now therefore hearken, O ye children. Oh ! happy moment, when the soul is made " willing in the day of his power " (Ps. xc. 3) ; when " the bands of love are drawing " (Hos. xi. 4) unto him ! The cold, dead indifference is gone. The enmity is slain. And who will not now joyfully swear fealty ; yea, count it his unspeakable delight to take such a yoke ; to be bound to such a service, where there is nothing but for our good ? (Deut. x. 12, 13.) Oh, my Prince — my Saviour ! thou hast based thy dominion on thy blood. Thou hast purchased thy right by thy cross. (1 Cor. vi. 19, 20. Rom. xiv. 9.) Thou rulest, only that thou mightest save. Take to thyself the glory of thy victory. I am thine — not my own — for ever.

34. *Blessed is the man that heareth me, watching daily at my gates, waiting at the posts of my doors.* 35. *For whoso findeth me, findeth life, and shall obtain favour of the Lord.* 36. *But he that sinneth against me wrongeth his own soul: all they that hate me love death.*

This is the *hearing* of faith — the voice of Christ to the inmost ear — the impression of his word upon the heart. (John, v. 25. Rev. iii. 20.) The effect is unwearied diligence and patient expectation; like the *priest* waiting *at the doors* of the tabernacle for the assured blessing (Exod. xxix. 42) ; or the people *watching at. the temple gates* for his return from his holy ministrations. (Luke, i. 10, 21.) This free and habitual attendance upon Sacred Ordinances indicates an healthy appetite for Divine nutriment. The superficial professor excuses himself from this " weariness " (Mal. i. 13) by the fear of legality, or the danger of *overvaluing* the means. But is there not at least equal danger of *undervaluing* the means, to which our gracious Lord has engaged his blessing ? (Exod. xx. 24. Isa. lvi. 7. Matt. xviii. 20.) In gazing on the heavenly Jerusalem, the Apostle " saw no temple therein." (Rev. xxi. 22.) But what right-hearted Christian will doubt that the life-blood of his soul while on earth consists in *watching*, like the servants of the temple, *daily at her gates* (Ps. lxxxiv. 1, 4, 10), *when not involving the neglect of imperative obligations.* Wisdom's child will ever be familiar with *Wisdom's gates.* The *Weekly* as well as the Sabbath assemblies will be his delight. Most thankful will he be for the service, which invigorates him in the midst of the toils of his worldly calling. " The way by the footsteps of the flock, *beside the Shepherds' tents*," will be his constant resort. (Cant. i. 7, 8.) And never would he wound the feelings of his Shepherd by wilfully absenting himself from the well, when he comes to water his flock. All the ordinances of prayer, meditation, Scripture reading, or godly conference, will be his salutary provision. When it is not so ; when the common routine satisfies ; when the intervals between the Sabbath pass without any appetite for food, or any effort to seek the bread of the sanctuary — Christian, is not thy pulse beating feebly ? Hast thou not lost many a precious message from thy Lord (see John, xx. 19, 24) — the fruit of thy Minister's special study, a word of distinct application to thy state, and which might have guided and comforted thee to the end of thy days ? Oh, listen to thy Lord's rebuke — " Be watchful and strengthen the things that remain that are ready to die ?"*

Observe the *blessing* breathed down upon the Lord's waiting ones. They *find life.* (Isa. lv. 3. John, v. 24.) For he on whom they *wait* is the Author (John, i. 4 ; xi. 25 ; xiv. 6), the Dispenser (Ib. x. 10), the Keeper of life. (Col. iii. 3. 1 John, v. 11. Jude, 1.) " He therefore that hath him, hath life " (1 John, v. 12), with all its present privileges of *favour of the Lord.* (Isa. lxiv. 5.) ' The smiles of God make heaven ; and they that *obtain favour of the Lord*, have a heaven upon earth.'† Set then this expectation before thine eyes in waiting on thy God. ' I am seeking *life* for my soul ; I will *wait at the post of his doors*, missing no opportunity of a means of grace ; I shall not wait in vain.'

Would that *the sinner* — the thoughtless sinner — not the daring and ungodly only — pondered how his heartless neglect of wisdom *wronged his own soul!* (Chap i. 17–19, 31 ; ix. 12. Jer. vii. 19. Acts, xiii. 46. Num. xvi. 38.) How cruel he is to himself, while he is despising his Saviour. Every bait of sin is the temptation to suicide — soul-murder. The snatching at it is as if men were in love with damnation. ' *They that hate me love death.* They love that which will be their death, and put that from them which would be their life. Sinners die, because they will die ; which leaves them inexcusable, makes their condemnation more intolerable, and will for ever justify God when he judges. " O Israel, thou hast destroyed thyself.'"‡

---

* Rev. iii. 2. 'The places where the Gospel is faithfully preached, are "the gates, and the posts of the doors of Wisdom," at which Christ would have his disciples to "wait daily." And may not Christians, consistently with other duties, redeem time for this waiting, as well as the children of this world find time for their vain amusements, who yet do not neglect *their* one thing needful? Is not the time spared from attending on a week-day, often spent in unprofitable visits or vain discourse? Ought Ministers to be "instant in season, and out of season," in preaching the word ; and ought not the people to be glad of an opportunity of hearing it?'—SCOTT.

† Lawson (George) Exposition of Proverbs. 2 vols. 12mo. 1821.

‡ Hos. xiii. 9 Henry *in loco.*

CHAPTER IX.

1. *Wisdom* [a] *hath builded her house, she hath hewn out her seven pillars:*
2. *She hath killed her beasts;* † *she hath mingled her wine; she hath also furnished her table.* 3. *She hath sent forth her maidens: she crieth upon the highest places of the city.* 4. *Whoso is simple, let him turn in hither: as for him that wanteth understanding, she saith to him,*
5. *Come, eat of my bread, and drink of the wine which I have mingled.*
6. *Forsake the foolish, and live; and go in the way of understanding.*

WE have delighted to contemplate the Divine Saviour in his glorious majesty, and specially in his wondrous love to *the sons of men.* (Chap. viii. 22–31.) Here his love is poured out before us. The parable of the marriage-feast clearly identifies the speaker. Then the King made the feast, and sent his servants to invite the guests. (Matt. xxii. 1–4, also Luke, xiv. 16, 17.) Here *Wisdom* is a Queen, according to Eastern custom, attended by *her maidens* (Exod. ii. 5. Esth. iv. 4), and *she sends them forth* to bid to the feast. *She hath builded her house—* " the church of the living God"— firm upon the *pillars* of eternal truth. (1 Tim. iii. 15. Eph. ii. 20–22. Heb. iii. 3, 4. Matt. xvi. 18.) The great sacrifice supplies her feast. (1 Cor. v. 7. Ps. xxxvi. 8. Isa. xxv. 6.) She *hath killed her beasts, mingled her wine* with the choicest spices,‡ and plentifully *furnished her table.* And now *she cries to the simple*—ignorant of his danger (Chap. xxii. 3), and easily deceived (Chap. xiv. 15) —to *him that wanteth understanding* (Hos. vii. 11)—who has no apprehension of his need, or desire for the blessing—*Let him turn in hither.* Here is a feast, not to see, but to enjoy. *Come, eat of the bread* of life; *drink of the wine* of gospel grace and joy.§ Is there not besides a special invitation for her children—*a table* richly *furnished* for their refreshment; where they *eat of the bread, and drink of the wine,* such as " the world know not of? " (Matt. xxvi. 26–28.)

But are not all comers welcome to the Gospel feast? The Master's heart flows along with every offer of his grace. His servants are ministers of reconciliation. (2 Cor. v. 18–20.) Their message is to tell of the bounty of Messiah's house, and to bid sinners welcome to Him. Here, sinner, is thy warrant—not thy worthiness, but thy need, and the invitation of thy Lord. All the blessings of his Gospel are set before thee—love without beginning, end, or change. Honour the freeness of his mercy. Let him have the full glory of his own grace,

---

* Wisdoms. Heb. Comp. note Chap i. 20.   † Comp. Gen. xliii. 16. Marg.

‡ Bishop Lowth remarks the difference between the Classics and the Hebrews The one by *mingled wine* understand wine diluted with water; the other intend wine made stronger by spices, or other exhilarating ingredients. Note on Isa. i. 22. Comp. chap. xxiii. 29–31. Cant. viii. 2.

§ Matt. xxii. 4. Isa. lv. 1. Comp. Bishop Hall's note.

who invites thee to a feast, when he might have frowned thee to hell.[*]
Let his heavenly hope be enthroned in the soul, displacing every subordinate object from its hold on thine affections, eclipsing the glories of
this present world, absorbing thy whole mind, consecrating thy whole
heart.

Here only are the ways of peace. The very severities of the Gospel
prepare the way for its consolations. But never can these blessings be
valued, till the path of *the foolish be forsaken.* Thou must *forsake*
either them or Christ. (Jam. iv. 4.) To abide with them, is to " remain
in the congregation of the dead." (Chap. xxi. 16.) To *forsake them,* is
the way of *life and understanding.* (Chap. xiii. 20. Ps. xxvi. 3–6 ; xxxiv.
12–14 ; cxix. 115. Amos, v. 15.) Are they more to you than salvation ?
To " be the friend of the world is to be the enemy of God." " Come
out, and be separate, and touch not the unclean thing ; and I will
receive thee, saith the Lord Almighty." (2 Cor. vi. 17, 18.)

7. *He that reproveth a scorner getteth to himself shame : and he that rebuketh*
   a wicked man getteth himself a blot. 8. *Reprove not a scorner, lest he*
   hate thee : rebuke a wise man, and he will love thee. 9. *Give instruc-*
   tion to a wise man, and he will yet be wiser : teach a just man, and he
   will increase in learning.

Wisdom's messengers must discriminate in the proclamation of their
message. If *the simple* welcome it, the *scorner and wicked* will rebel.
Yet we must distinguish between the ignorant and the wilful *scorner.*
Paul " did it ignorantly, in unbelief." (1 Tim. i. 13.) His countrymen
deliberately refused the blessing, and shut themselves out from the free
offers of salvation. (Acts, xiii. 45, 46, 50 ; xviii. 6. Matt. x. 14, 15.)

One cannot think of the scorner without compassion. He cannot
bear to commune with himself. Under an assumed gaiety, he would
envy — as did Colonel Gardiner — the dog his existence. ' I hate life '
— said Voltaire — ' yet I am afraid to die.' Such is the bitterness of
soul linked with rebellion against God ! Wretched indeed must he be,
when the thought of God is an abomination, and when it is necessary
to his peace to expunge all idea of him from his creed. (Ps. xiv. 1.)

Yet, in dealing with him, Solomon here gives us the rule of Christian
prudence. The gospel is a thing too holy to be exposed to scoffing
fools. (Matt. vii. 6.) Why should we *reprove,* where more harm than
good may be occasioned? Avoid irritations. Await the favourable
opportunity. Sometimes a sad, serious, intelligible silence is the most
effective reproof. (Amos, v. 13 ; vi. 10.) Whereas open *rebuke* might
stir up a torrent of *hatred* (Chap. xv. 12 ; xxiii. 9. 1 Kings, xxii. 8.

---

[*] Calvin speaks of the pleading invitations of Christ, as ' his sweet and more than
motherly allurements,' and beautifully adds—that ' the word of God is never opened to us,
but that he with a motherly sweetness opens his own bosom to us.' On Matt. xxiii. 37.

2 Chron. xxv. 16) and abuse (Gen. xix. 9. Amos, vii. 10. Matt. vii. 6) ; and under provocation of spirit, the *reprover* might *get to himself a blot.* (Isa. xxix. 21.)

Yet this prudence must not degenerate into cowardice, and compromise the primary obligation boldly to rebuke sin (Eph. v. 11. 1 Thess. v. 14. 1 Tim. v. 20. Matt. xiv. 3, 4), and confess our Master. (Matt. x. 32, 33. Acts, iv. 19, 20.) Every sinner is not *a scorner.* And a "word spoken in due season, how good is it!" (Chap. xv. 23.) That false delicacy, therefore, which recoils from an unflinching profession, is treachery to our Lord, and deep—perhaps eternal—injury to our fellow-sinners. Have not each of us a tongue to speak ? To suffer any therefore to rush into perdition without opening our mouths to save them, is a sin of omission, which will cause a bitter pang to the awakened conscience.

The *wise and just man* gladly encourages well-timed reproof. (Chap. xxviii. 23.) Conscious of his own failings, he *loves his reprover* as a friend to his best interest (Lev. xix. 17. Ps. cxli. 5. 1 Sam. xxv. 33. 2 Sam. xii. 7–14) ; and he would receive *instruction* from the lowest, as a means of becoming *yet wiser, and increasing in learning.* (Chap. i. 5. Exod. xviii. 17–24. Acts, xviii. 26.)

After all—wisely to give, and humbly to receive, reproof, requires much prayer, self-denial, love, and sincerity. But where the mind of Christ is mutually exhibited, it cements a bond of the warmest affection. (1 Sam. xxv. 32–42.) "Faithful are the wounds of a friend." (Chap. xxvii. 6.) Happy is that church which receives the loving admonitions of the Christian pastor with humility and thankfulness.°

10. *The fear of the Lord is the beginning of wisdom : and the knowledge of the holy is understanding.* 11. *For by me thy days shall be multiplied, and the years of thy life shall be increased.*

The repetition of this weighty sentence (Chap. i. 7. Job, xxviii. 28. Ps. cxi. 10) deepens our estimate of its importance. *The fear of the Lord* was a lovely grace in the perfect humanity of Jesus. (Isa. xi. 2, 3.) Let it be the test of our "predestination to be conformed to his image." (Rom. viii. 29.) It is the genuine spirit of adoption. The child of God has only one dread—to offend his Father ; only one desire—to please and delight in him. Thus is *the fear of the Lord* connected with his love. 'The heart that is touched with the loadstone of Divine love, trembles still with godly fear.'† If this temper is *the beginning,* it is

---

* 2 Cor. ii. 1-9. Mr. Martyn—his Biographer observes—'felt reproof to be 'a duty of unlimited extent and almost insuperable difficulty.' But, said he, 'the way to know when to address men, and when to abstain, is to love.' And, as love is most genuine, where the heart is most abased, he resolved not to reprove others, when he could conscientiously be silent, except he experienced at the same time a peculiar contrition of spirit.'—Life, chap. ii.

† Leighton on 1 Pet. ii. 17.

also (as the word imports) *the head—of wisdom*—not only its first rudiment, but its matured exercise. It is obviously combined with *the knowledge of the Holy One.*° For if men did but know *his holiness*— "who would not fear thee, O Lord?" (Rev. xv. 4.) *Days multiplied* were the Old Testament reward. (Chap. iii. 2, 16; iv. 10; x. 27.) And truly the value of life is only realized in the *knowledge* and service of God. Inconceivably joyous to us is the prospect of *years of life increased* into a boundless eternity—infinite desires; fully satisfied, yet excited unceasingly to more full and heavenly enjoyment.

12. *If thou be wise, thou shalt be wise for thyself: but if thou scornest, thou alone shalt bear it.*

The consequences of our conduct, good or bad, chiefly reflect on ourselves. (Chap. xvi. 26.) God cannot be profited by us (Job, xxii. 2, 3. Ps. xvi. 2. Luke, xvii. 10); and he is infinitely above our injury. (Job, xxxv. 6, 7.) *The wise* man's light is a blessing to the Church and to the world. (Matt. v. 14, 16.) But he *is wise for himself*—for his own advantage. (Chap. iii. 13–18; xxiv. 3. Eccles. viii. 1.) *The scorner* is a grief to his minister, and a stumbling to his church. But he hurts no one so much as himself. *He alone shall bear it.* (Chap. viii. 36. Ezek. xviii. 20. Luke, vii. 30.) A surety indeed there is. But *his scorning* rejects him. He sinks therefore into perdition under a millstone of guilt without remedy. (Chap. xxix. 1. Heb. x. 28, 29. Lev. xxiv. 15.) This then is the ordinance of God. "Every man shall bear his own burden. Whatsoever a man soweth, that shall he also reap:" life or death—a double harvest—for time and for eternity. (Gal. vi. 5, 7, 8.)

13. *A foolish woman is clamorous; she is simple, and knoweth nothing.*
14. *For she sitteth at the door of her house, on a seat in the high places of the city.* 15. *To call passengers who go right on their ways:*
16. *Whoso is simple, let him turn in hither: and as for him that wanteth understanding, she saith to him,* 17. *Stolen waters are sweet, and bread eaten in secret* (of secresies, marg.) *is pleasant.* 18. *But he knoweth not that the dead are there; and that her guests are in the depths of hell.*

Wisdom's free and gracious invitation has been before us   And we

---

° The parallelism with the former clause seems to demand this meaning. The application of the plural number to the sacred name is elsewhere used by Solomon (verse i. 1-20. Eccles. xii. 1) as well as by others of the inspired Writers. Gen. i. 26. Job, xxxv. 10. Isa. liv. 5. Compare the Heb. of Hos. xii. 1. Josh. xxiv. 19. Bishop Horsley remarks— God is the only Being, to whom the same name in the singular and in the plural may be indiscriminately applied. And this change from the one number to the other, without any thing in the principles of language to account for it, is frequent in speaking of God in the Hebrew tongue, but unexampled in the case of any other Being.' Sermon xxix. on the Watchers. The reason of this peculiar usage—we may add—is obvious to any one, who receives with implicit and reverential faith the Scriptural revelation of the Divine Essence.

might almost ask — who could resist it? Now we have an allurement from the opposite quarter. For sin is no less earnest to destroy, than wisdom is to save. The distinct character of folly here alluded to, may be gathered from the pictures formerly given. (Chap. ii. v. vii.) Fleshly lusts are in open opposition to Divine wisdom. 'The delight of the soul fixed on anything but God and his grace, is but spiritual adultery.'* *The woman of foolishness is clamorous* (Chap. vii. 11), and, though "subtil in heart" (Ib. verse 10) in the devices of Satan, she is *simplicity* itself in her utter ignorance of right. So fearfully do sensual pleasures darken the understanding, that the tempter, from the very habit of deceiving, becomes the victim of her own delusion! (Hos. iv. 11. 2 Tim. iii. 13.) With a shameless front she dares to present herself *in the highest places of the city* (Gen. xxxviii. 14, 21. Jer. iii. 2, 3. Ezek. xvi. 24, 25, 31), alluring, not only those who are "going the way to her house" (Chap. vii. 8), but the inexperienced who are *going right on their ways.* Thus, even the highway of God, though a path of safety (Chap. x. 9), is beset with temptation. Satan is so angry with none as with those, *who are going right on.* When Israel was in the straight path, quickly did he turn them aside by the golden calf. (Exod. xxiv. 7, with xxxii.) And now enticements or assaults wait on every step. The temptation to open sin would be revolting. But must you give up all your pleasures? May not some *stolen waters* (Chap. v. 15–17. 2 Sam. xi. 2), some *secret* indulgences (Chap. xx. 17. Job, xx. 12–14), be allowed? Ah! sinner — there is no such thing as *secret* sin. All is naked and open as day before the eye of God. (Job, xxiv. 15; xxxiv. 21, 22.) All will soon be proclaimed before the assembled world. (Luke, xii. 1, 2.) But the strength of this temptation is, that they are forbidden pleasures. (Gen. iii. 1–6.) Restraint provokes the dormant power of sin;† as children will do that which is forbidden, *because* it is forbidden. But what will be the end? Satan shows only the sparkling cup, and the glaring light. Ask to look into the inner chamber. The blinded fool hath wilfully closed his eyes (Chap. vii. 22. Isa. i. 3. 2 Pet. iii. 5); else might he *know that the dead are there; and that her guests* — the wilful despisers of wisdom, are *in the very depths of hell.* (Chap. ii. 18; vii. 27.)

Reader — *the wisdom of God,* and the great deceiver of man — stand

---

* Diodati.

† Rom. vii. 8. 1 Cor. xv. 56. See Augustine's description of his robbing the pear-tree — not for the gain of the fruit (the greater part of which he threw away), but for the mere pleasure of sin *as sin — as breaking God's law.* Truly affecting also is it to see him, like the Psalmist (Ps. li. 5) tracing the sin to its root — 'Behold my heart, O Lord, behold my heart, which thou hadst pity upon in the very bottom of the bottomless pit!'—*Confess.* iii. 4, 6.

> ' Nitimur in vetitum semper, cupimusque negata :
>   Sic interdictis imminet æger aquis.
> Quidquid servatur, cupimus magis, ipsaque furem
>   Cura vocat, pauci, quod sinet alter, amant.'—OVID.

before you.   Both are wooing thine heart; the one for life—the other
for death.   Both are intensely anxious for success.   *Wisdom crieth.
The foolish woman is clamorous.* (Verse 3 with 13.)   Both take their
station *in the high places of the city.* (Verse 3 with 15.)   Both spread
out their feast *for the simple* and ignorant (Verse 4 with 16), smiling
and happy on the brink of ruin.   But how opposite their end?   The
one makes *the simple* wise unto eternal life.   The other bears away her
willing captive into unutterable misery.   Which voice arrests thine
ear, and allures thine heart?   Which feast excites thine appetite?
Whose *guest* art thou?   Wilt thou not open thine eyes to the infatuation and pollution of this house of horror and death?   Oh! remember
that every listening to the enticement rivets thy chain, rejoices thy
grand enemy, cheats thee out of thy present, no less than of thine
eternal, happiness, and will banish thee for ever from the paradise re-
opened as thy home.   Thou mayest sink into the grave and perish.
But it will be with the Saviour's voice crying in thine ears, " How long,
ye *simple* ones, will ye love *simplicity?*" (Chap. i. 22.)   The voice of
mercy now warns thee against estranging thyself from thy God.   But
mercy is limited to time.   Then justice, without mercy, will hold the
scales with relentless severity, and the sentence of condemnation will
bind thee in the lost and blasted kingdom of eternal death.   What
then is our heart's desire and prayer, but the free grace and love of the
Gospel may draw and fix thine heart; and that the Lord may preserve
thee from the tempter's snare, by keeping thee closely walking with
himself.

An Address

To

YOUNG PERSONS

After

CONFIRMATION

By Rev. Charles Bridges

REVISED BY THE EXECUTIVE COMMITTEE OF "THE PROTESTANT EPISCOPAL
SOCIETY FOR THE PROMOTION OF EVANGELICAL KNOWLEDGE"

1853

THE ADDRESS

You have now "avouched"–or publicly professed–"the Lord to be your God."[1] You have entered the fight against all the Lord's enemies and the enemies of your soul; you have engaged to renounce and resist them; and to "walk in all the commandments of God."

In your Baptism, a believing hope was expressed, "that you would not be ashamed to confess the Faith of Christ crucified, and manfully to fight under his Banner against Sin, the World, and the Devil, and to continue Christ's faithful soldier and servant unto your life's end."[2] You have repeatedly laid claim to this character in your Catechism; and at length you have come forward to declare in the face of the Church, and in the teeth of the World, that the cross of Christ is your boast and glory; that you disown all other Masters; and desire to live only in the service and to the praise of your Redeemer.

Let me, however, solemnly remind you, that this declaration is *for ever.*[3] It is an engagement; or rather the open profession of a former engagement, made between God and yourself; and every future moment of your life is to be a part of the fulfillment of it. This at least is certain, that every moment must, and will be, either the fulfillment, or the breach of it. You are every moment assaulted by some of the enemies of your soul; every moment either the faith you professed is encouraging you to resist them; or, in the neglect of this faith, you are tamely yielding to them. Every moment some part of the will and commands of God is to be done, or submitted to: and every moment you are either "constrained by the love of Christ" to do or to suffer that will; or you are shrinking from it, and so "denying the Lord that bought you."

How clear is it—not only from reason and Scripture, but from the language of our own Church, that the vow you have taken upon yourselves, binds you for ever to the love and service of God! Your renouncing of the World, the Flesh, and the Devil, is spoken of as a determination never "to follow, nor be led by them," "to *crucify* the old man, and *utterly abolish* the whole body of sin," *continually* to mortify

---

[1] Deuteronomy 26:17.
[2] Baptismal Service
[3] See Jeremiah 50:5.

all your evil and corrupt affections. The faith you have professed is "*constantly* to believe in God;" and the obedience you have promised is "to walk in God's will and commandments *unto your life's end.*" [4]

Confirmation, therefore, seriously undertaken may be with you the first step of your heavenly journey; and the whole journey is only a repetition of such steps, one every moment of your life till you come to the end. You have thrown down your challenge to the enemies of God: and your after life is the fight that follows that challenge. For you have drawn the sword, and thrown away the scabbard; and you can never quit the field, while life lasts, without giving up the hopes, and losing the character of a Christian.

Now then the fight begins. At Baptism you were enlisted; at Confirmation you entered the field; and you are henceforth upon actual service, ready, God helping you, to "endure hardness, as a good soldier of Jesus Christ."[5]

I shall endeavor, under God's blessing, to show what you will want in beginning this warfare: and then give you some directions for holding on in it.

I. In entering upon the warfare,

1. *Let us attend to what the Scripture says of the spirit of the Gospel.* "They are not of the world, even as I am not of the world." "We walk by faith, not by sight." "As he is, so are we in this world." "Our conversation is in heaven." "We look not at the things which are seen, but at the things which are not seen." "For to me to live is Christ."[6] These are the principles of our Christian profession. They flow from a living faith in Jesus Christ our Savior. Under their blessed influence we "take unto us the whole armor of God that we may be able to withstand in the evil day, and, having done all, to stand."[7]

2. *Let us count the cost of this warfare.* "Because ye are not of the world, but I have chosen you out of the world, therefore the world hateth you." Because we "are called the sons of God, therefore the world knoweth us not because it knew him not." "As then, he that was horn after the flesh persecuted him that was born after the Spirit, even so it is now." "If ye live after the flesh ye shall die; but if ye through the Spirit do mortify the deeds of the body, ye shall live." "Your adversary the Devil, as a roaring lion, walketh about, seeking whom he may devour; whom resist, steadfast in the faith." "He that loveth father, or mother more than me, is not worthy

---

[4] Baptismal Service and Catechism
[5] 2 Timothy 2:3
[6] John 17:14; 2 Corinthians 5:7; 1 John 4:17; Philippians 3:20; 2 Cor. 4:18; Phil. 1:21
[7] Ephesians 6:13

of me; and he that loveth son or daughter more than me, is not worthy of me." "He that findeth his life shall lose it; and he that loseth his life for my sake shall find it."[8]

The Scripture speaks of this warfare in the same way in which it appears in the Baptismal vow. I mean "This is the victory that overcometh the world, even our faith,"—faith, which "believes the love which God has to you;" faith, which attaches, and devotes the believer to the Lord Jesus; and which draws continual supplies of grace from him, to "fight this good fight," even unto the end. It was "by faith Moses, when he was come to years, refused to be called the son of Pharaoh's daughter; choosing rather to suffer affliction with the people of God, than to enjoy the pleasures of sin for a season; esteeming the reproach of Christ greater riches than the treasures in Egypt; for he had respect unto the recompense of the reward. By faith he forsook Egypt, not fearing the wrath of the king; for he endured, as seeing him who is invisible." By faith Abraham was enabled to give up the dearest comforts of life, and to follow at the command of God, "not knowing whither he went." And "we are compassed about with a great cloud of witnesses," who look down upon us from Heaven; and with one voice encourage us to "run the" same "race set before us, looking unto" the same Savior—"Jesus, the author and finisher of our faith."[9]

And now let me ask—What has your own experience taught you respecting the Scriptural account of this matter? I mean—your experience during the short time since you have put on the "armor of God," and entered by profession into the field of battle? Remember what has been already noticed—there is not a moment since your Confirmation, that your enemies have not been fighting against you. The *enemy of souls* has been endeavoring to draw you back from strict fidelity to God; tempting you to put a false meaning upon your vow, whenever you have been called upon to perform it; aggravating the difficulties and dangers of a life of self-denial; setting forth the charms of worldly objects, and the pleasure of careless ease. *The world too* has been spreading itself before your sight, while the Devil was commending it to your heart; or, if you have stood a little firm against its pleasures, it has perhaps assailed you with scorn and mockery; at least with the coolness and neglect of those, from whom you had expected kindness, and from whom, till now, you had received it. But above all—*the flesh*. The Devil may not, the world cannot, always tempt. But no waking moment

[8] John 15:19; 1 John 3:2; Galatians 4:29; Romans 8:13; 1 Peter 5:8,9; Matthew 10:37,39
[9] 1 John 5:4; Hebrews 11:8,24-27; 12:2

can be free from the influence of "the imagination of the thoughts of the heart, which are only evil continually."[10] Even where the Spirit dwells in the heart, "the flesh will always be lusting against it."[11] While the Spirit is continually impressing your minds with the love, the majesty, the holiness, the grace, the tenderness of God in the gift of his Son, is not self always struggling for a little less constant watchfulness, a little rest to the flesh, a little less lively sense of the character and claims of God? Is not the heart sometimes ready to make even a desperate effort, and to say—"*I must be indulged; I will have my own way?*"

I do not ask, whether in this struggle you have always *conquered?* But I ask, and I wish you honestly to ask yourselves, have you always *fought?* I doubt not but you have met with many humbling proofs of the deceitfulness of your hearts. You have found that no dependence is to be placed on frames of mind, and impressions. You perhaps could not have thought that the desire, the delight, with which at Confirmation you seemed to devote yourselves to Him who died for you, could so soon have left your hearts cold and empty, as you have often felt them to be, since this solemn season of your dedication to God.

Now this is permitted, to show you what you are; to prevent you from placing reliance on any thing whatever, but Christ. It is to show you how weak you are, and where your strength lies; to stir you up to prayer, that God would fulfill his promises to you; that you may be enabled to say, not merely because you read it in the Scriptures, but because you can set your seal to it in your own case—"In the Lord have I righteousness and strength."[12] How blessed is the distinction between the believer, who has recourse by faith to this strength, and those who depend upon their own!—"The youths shall faint and be weary, and the young men shall utterly fall; but they that wait upon the Lord shall renew their strength: they shall mount up with wings as eagles; they shall run and not be weary; they shall walk, and not faint."[13]

Your experience in this respect will show you more clearly the meaning of that important text often quoted—"When I am weak, then am I strong."[14] Therefore let none of these things discourage you. Your vow, if you made it in dependence upon the grace of Christ, gave you a hold on Almighty strength. And if you sincerely

---

[10] Genesis 6:5
[11] Galatians 5:17
[12] Isaiah 45:24
[13] Isaiah 40:30,31
[14] 2 Corinthians 12:10

desire to "hold fast the profession of your faith," remember whom "you have believed," and let nothing persuade you to doubt "that he is able to keep that which you have committed to him against that day." "Greater is he that is in us, than he that is in the world."[15]

You will perhaps ask—what are those exertions and endeavors of faith, by which we are to maintain this habitual warfare against our enemies, and this persevering struggle to fulfill the will of God!

II. For this purpose I would offer the following directions.

1. *Never lose sight of the great object of faith.*

Faith is dependence. Its strength consists not in any peculiar power of its own, but is derived wholly from its object—Jesus Christ. Faith acts according to all the different circumstances of the believer, by means of the impressions, motives, and encouragements, which are drawn from a view of the Savior.

"They looked unto him and were lightened, and their faces were not ashamed." "Look unto me, and be ye saved, all the ends of the earth." "I live by the faith of the Son of God, who loved me, and gave himself for me." "Abide in me, and I in you. As the branch cannot bear fruit of itself, except it abide in the vine, no more can ye, except ye abide in me." "I can do all things through Christ, which strengtheneth me."[16]

Now let these texts set before you the completeness of Christ for all the wants of your soul—for all the purposes of God's mercy and grace in your salvation. *As to your ground of acceptance therefore*—be sure that it rests simply upon what Christ has done for you. If by faith you have an interest in him, "you are complete in him!"[17] and therefore you need nothing in yourselves; no frames and feelings—no prayers, duties, or repentance—to recommend you to God. Under all circumstances of trial, weakness, difficulty, and temptation, you must go on to the end, "beholding the Lamb of God, which taketh away the sin of the world:"[18] pleading his blood which pleads for you with everlasting merit; thus making him and his work "all your salvation."

And so as to your sanctification—"All your springs are in him," He "is made unto you Sanctification," as well as "Righteousness."[19] You must not look for your sanctification to arise from any train of feelings or duties. It shows itself indeed in

---

[15] 2 Corinthians 12:10; 2 Timothy 1:12; 1 John 4:4
[16] Psalm 34:5; Isaiah 45:22; Galatians 2:20; John 15:4; Philippians 4:13
[17] Colossians 2:10
[18] John 1:29
[19] Psalm 87:7; 1 Corinthians 1:30

all the practical exercises of our high profession; but it flows immediately from Christ. Union with him is your life; and until you have found life in him, all your works are "dead works;"[20] hateful to God, and every way unfit for his service.

Then as for your strength—it is "his strength" in you "made perfect in weakness." And here indeed is all the comfort you want. Weak as you are, and difficult as is your work, you look to one who, when you are "oppressed," has engaged to "undertake for you;"[21] in whom "it hath pleased the Father that all fullness should dwell," on purpose that "of his fullness you might receive grace for grace."[22] He knows the grace you want, and he has promised that his "grace shall be sufficient for you."[23] He has laid by your portion for every day, and keeps it for you till the moment when it is required. He undertook for you on the cross, when he "his own self bore our sins in his own body on the tree."[24] He undertakes for you now, when he "appears in the presence of God for you,"[25] and receives on your behalf the gifts you stand in need of.[26]—Thus on every account you see the importance of never losing sight of this glorious object of your faith. Now, in order that you may keep him always in view, I would next say—

2. *Search the Scriptures daily.*

The grand reason for this search is—that "they testify of him."[27] Faith there finds what she is in search of—the history of the life, death, and doctrine of "God manifest in the flesh;"[28] and the claims, encouragements, and supports, which the Spirit of God, speaking of the salvation of Christ, furnishes to our souls. The principal of these are summed up in the creed, which is therefore called "the Articles of the Christian Faith." The Creed will help you in searching the Scriptures, because it is a short account of all he did and suffered, and of what he is doing now for your salvation.

What can be more solemn, and yet more encouraging, than such passages of Scripture as these "Ye are not your own, for ye are bought with a price; therefore glorify God in your body, and in your spirit, which are God's." "That I may know him, and the power of

---

[20] Hebrews 6:1; 9:14
[21] Isaiah 38:14
[22] Colossians 1:19; John 1:16
[23] 2 Corinthians 12:9
[24] 1 Peter 2:24
[25] Hebrews 9:24
[26] Psalm 68:18
[27] John 5:39
[28] 1 Timothy 3:16

his resurrection, and the fellowship of his sufferings, being made conformable unto his death."[29] "Who was delivered for our offences and raised again for our justification."[30] "Seek those things that are above, where Christ sitteth at the right hand of God." "If any man sin, we have an advocate with the Father, Jesus Christ the righteous: and he is the propitiation for our sins."[31] "We must all appear before the judgment-seat of Christ."[32] "If ye love me, keep my commandments. And I will pray the Father, and he shall give you another Comforter, that he may abide with you for ever: even the Spirit of truth, whom the world cannot receive."[33] " If we confess our sins, he is faithful and just to forgive us our sins, and to cleanse us from all unrighteousness."[34] "Be thou faithful unto death: and I will give thee a crown of life."[35]

Let no day pass without attentively reading such passages as those. Dwell on them, and wait in hope for that impression on your heart, which a spiritual understanding of the character and offices of the Lord Jesus will give you. Remember, every thing that you get of Christ is pure gold. Every fresh view of his glory, every new thought of his love, is worth all the treasures of the world to you. Come then to the cross, and abide there. See what was done there; and what it was done for, and what it has delivered us from; and what tempers, and what conduct it was intended to produce in us. And then let faith lift up her eyes, and behold Jesus sitting, and pleading at the right hand of God, and preparing a place of eternal blessedness for them that love him.

But it is not enough that we understand what we read. It is written, "They shall be all taught of God."[36] He only can teach the heart, and therefore he only can "teach us to profit." While we read the Scriptures,—

3. *We must also add frequent and earnest prayer for the Holy Spirit.* We see how David prayed for Divine teaching, that he might profit by the word, as well as understand it. "Open thou mine eyes, that I may behold wondrous things out of thy law." "I am a stranger in the earth; hide not thy commandments from me." "I will run the

---

[29] 1 Corinthians 6:19,20; Philippians 3:10. "Who was crucified, dead and buried." (Creed)

[30] Romans 4:25. "The third day he rose again from the dead." (Creed)

[31] Colossians 3:1; 1 John 2:1. "He ascended into Heaven, and sitteth on the right hand of God the Father Almighty." (Creed)

[32] 2 Corinthians 5:10. "He shall come to judge the quick and the dead." (Creed)

[33] John 14:15-17. "I believe in the Holy Ghost." (Creed)

[34] 1 John 1:9. "The forgiveness of sins." (Creed)

[35] Revelation 2:10. "And the life everlasting." (Creed)

[36] John 6:45, with Isaiah 54:13

way of thy commandments, when thou shalt enlarge my heart." "Teach me, O Lord, the way of thy statutes; and I shall keep it unto the end." "I have not departed from thy judgments, for thou hast taught me." "Teach me to do thy will, for thou art my God: thy Spirit is good; lead me into the land of uprightness."[37]

You must not expect to derive any benefit from the word of God, but by the Spirit of God. You must therefore pray for yourselves, as Paul prayed for the Ephesians—that God "would give unto you the Spirit of wisdom and revelation in the knowledge of him, the eyes of your understanding being enlightened: that you may know what is the hope of his calling, and what the riches of the glory of his inheritance in the saints, and what is the exceeding greatness of his power to us who believe, according to the working of his mighty power."[38] Thus you will be led to consider spiritual things, and spiritual truths, not merely as being real, but more than that—of unspeakable importance and value; you will feel the reproofs of the Scriptures, take heed to their directions, lean on their support, and revive by their consolations: you will not only hear of Christ as a Savior, but will constantly flee to him as *your* Savior. While he invites like the parent bird,[39] so do you fly to him, as the helpless brood to the wings of their mother on every approach of danger—feeling your present, urgent distress—and humbly trusting in his protection.

As this becomes the habit of your soul, you will more and more enjoy that "peace with God through our Lord Jesus Christ,"[40] which will strengthen you to maintain the Christian character and to carry on the Christian warfare to the end.

4. *Set the Savior always before you as your pattern.* He "left us an example, that we should follow his steps."[41] Learn from him, what is very important, that when we renounce the world, we do not renounce lawful business and necessary engagements in the world: nor the duties which we owe to our parents and relations. Follow him, who taught you the duties of children by being "subject to his parents;"[42] who was fearless in the cause of God, while he "submitted to every ordinance of man for the Lord's sake." Let the love of Christ be your motive, the example of Christ your pattern, and the strength and grace of Christ your dependence, in all the

---

[37] Psalm 119:18,19,32,33,102; 143:10
[38] Ephesians 1:17-19
[39] Matthew 23:37
[40] Romans 5:1
[41] 1 Peter 2:21
[42] Luke 2:51

duties of relative and social life. Then your love to those who are already dear to you will be more powerful, refined, and lasting: then you will act towards them with affection and respect without selfishness. You will also be cheerful, and ready to maintain universal kindness, delighting in the happiness, and endeavoring to promote the comfort of all, and "especially of those who are of the household of faith."[43] For, while you pay particular attention to your relative duties, you must be gentle and kind to all. "As you have opportunity," "in meekness instruct those that oppose themselves; if peradventure God will give them repentance to the acknowledging of the truth." "And be ready always to give an answer to every one that asketh you a reason of the hope that is in you, with meekness and fear."[44] Especially let your example speak; "that if any obey not the word, they may without a word be won, while they behold your" upright "conversation coupled with" godly "fear."[45]

But more especially let the love and example of Christ influence your conduct and temper towards each other, and towards all who love "the truth as it is in Jesus." Lay aside all contention about little indifferent matters, and doubtful uncertain questions. Be not on the watch to discover who is right and who is wrong, nor to make any person "an offender far a word."—"Receive one another, as Christ also received us, to the glory of God."[46] A regard to this important rule may often show that both are right, when both were thinking each other wrong. Let this tenderness of Christ; therefore be your daily pattern. Be kindly watchful for each other's comfort, ready to listen and help in each other's difficulties. Be upright, cheerful, sincere—"by love serving one another;"[47] and yet so combining Christian love with faithfulness to your Master, that, while you preserve charity, you may make no sacrifice of truth.

Thus fighting in your Savior's strength, as the Captain of your salvation, against all his and your enemies; and "abstaining from those things which war against the soul," you will, "by well-doing put to silence the ignorance of foolish men,"[48] and also become the Lord's honored instruments in leading those to Christ, who are yet strangers to his grace; and in strengthening those, who are already under its influence.

---

[43] Galatians 6:10
[44] 1 Timothy 2:25; 1 Peter 3:15;
[45] 1 Peter 3:1,2
[46] Romans 15:7
[47] Galatians 5:13
[48] 1 Peter 2:11,15

And now, if you not only "believe in the Lord Jesus in your heart," but have also "with the mouth made confession unto salvation;"[49] we invite you after due consideration, prayer, and instruction, to follow up your public confession, by coming to the table of the Lord. There "by showing forth the Lord's death,"[50] you will profess before the world and the Church that you are not ashamed of his Cross, that you are ready to "go forth without the camp, bearing his reproach."[51] By taking upon yourselves the badge of his profession, you will show that you honor him as your Master, remember him as your Friend, and trust in him as your Savior. This is also a duty you owe to your fellow-Christians, "with one mind," and one profession, "striving together for the faith of the Gospel."[52] We must therefore "stand in doubt of you," if you willfully draw back from this pledge of union with Christ and his people. It shows a neglect of the authority of your Divine Master—the power of unbelief—the fear of the cross—and a want of love to Christ and to his poor despised people. On the other hand, by attending upon this holy ordinance, you will renew from time to time your confirmation vow; the remembrance of your Savior's love will more and more "constrain you;" and you will find the benefit of the "strengthening and refreshing of your soul by the body and blood of Christ."[53]

Do you then desire to come to his table? In his name we affectionately bid you welcome, "Eat, O friends, yea drink abundantly, O beloved."[54] Here is "meat to eat, which the world knoweth not of." Your Savior's "flesh is meat indeed, and his blood drink indeed."[55] "Go in the strength of that meat"[56] to your daily work, and your daily conflict, rejoicing in the Lord. Thus you will form a closer union with the people of God, who will rejoice to add you to their society, separated from the world, and journeying towards heaven; and who will be ever ready to "strengthen your weak hands and confirm your feeble knees"[57] in the ways of God.

In conclusion, I would address a few words distinctly to different classes of young persons.

---

[49] Romans 10:9,10
[50] 1 Corinthians 11:26
[51] Hebrews 13:13
[52] Philippians 1:27
[53] See the Catechism
[54] Song of Solomon 5:1
[55] John 6:55
[56] 1 Kings 19:8
[57] Isaiah 35:3; cf. Hebrews 12:12

I. *There are some, who do not, I fear, see the engagement of Confirmation in its full extent, particularly with respect to the renouncing of the world.* Yet they regard the vow, as far as they allow it to extend, as of very solemn importance. Wherever there is this honest, and—as I would hope in many cases—Divine impression, let me suggest the Scriptural advice—"Hold fast that thou hast." "Grow in grace, and in the knowledge of our Lord and Savior Jesus Christ."[58] This knowledge will draw you out of the world without the persuasion of man;[59] just as the merchantman gladly gave up his "goodly pearls," when the "pearl of great price" was set before him.[60] Remember the promises God has made to those, who diligently improve what they already have—"Then shall you know, if ye follow on to know the Lord." "Unto every one that hath shall be given, and he shall have abundance."[61] And seek the fulfillment of these promises in the diligent use of the means of grace. "Be sober, and watch unto prayer." "Search the Scriptures daily whether these things are so." "Take no commandments of men for doctrines," whether agreeing or disagreeing with your own feelings; "For one is your Master, even Christ." "There is one lawgiver, who is able to save, and to destroy."[62]

II. *There are others who freely acknowledge that they never considered the engagement made at Confirmation, as laying them under any obligation to a new life, or to any change whatever. And there are others again, who plainly show they think this, though they do not say it.* I am persuaded that in your state of mind no blessing can have been found in Confirmation; nor do I know what benefit can be expected to follow it; except indeed, that, by the remembrance of your willful act of solemn mockery, you may be pricked to the heart and brought upon your knees in secret, in "the Spirit of supplication to look on Him whom you have pierced, and mourn."[63] Then indeed, in the first tear of contrition, in the first cry of the heart for mercy, you will find the seal of tender love, and gracious acceptance. And aggravated as your guilt will then appear to you, nothing will be able to stop the full tide of forgiveness from flowing into your soul: for "though thy sins be as scarlet, they shall be as snow; though they be red like crimson, they shall be as wool."[64]

---

[58] Revelation 3:11; 2 Peter 3:18
[59] See Galatians 6:14; 1 John 5:4,5
[60] Compare Matthew 13:45,46 with Philippians 3:7,8
[61] Hosea 6:3; Matthew 25:29
[62] 1 Peter 4:7; Acts 17:11; Matthew 15:9; 23:8; James 4:12
[63] Zechariah 12:10
[64] Isaiah 1:18

III. *I would ask; are any of you who have lately "subscribed with your hands, unto the Lord," already tired of your choice?* Do you begin to think your vow less binding, less solemn, than it was at the time you made it? Does sin look more pleasant, and more inviting? Do the ways of God seem more strange and melancholy than they did? Have not you yet determined, whether you will renounce the world or Christ? A heart under the power of conviction is only half won—still kept in bondage the world loved and struggling for its mastery. A heart under the power of faith has burst the chains of sin and the world for ever. I say to you therefore—Believe, and live. "Resist the devil, steadfast in the faith, and he will flee from you."[65] But in your own delusions? Oh! beware, lest Satan should get an advantage of you, from your "being ignorant of his devices."[66] Be assured that sin is still as abominable, as you thought it to be, when you engaged to renounce it: the world is as deceitful and ruinous, and the lusts of the flesh as contrary to God, and as hurtful to your soul as ever. Fear then drawing back, worse than death; and remember that looking back is next to drawing back, and "drawing back" is the direct road to "perdition."[67] Pray that the Spirit may be poured upon you as "floods upon the dry ground." Then you will "grow as the willows by the water courses;" you will "subscribe with your" heart as well as your "hand unto the Lord."[68] You will not, you cannot *then* repent of your choice. You will only desire that fresh ties may bind you and fresh motives constrain you. Your language will be—"Thou hast loosed my bonds;"[69] bind me, O my Savior, with new bonds, that never shall be loosed: suffer not my wayward heart to stray even in thought, from thee and thy service; "teach me thy way, O Lord; I will walk in thy truth; unite my heart to fear thy name."[70]

IV. *Most of you are young in years: and even those who are sincere, are many of you young in grace and knowledge.* You know but little yet of the difficulties or the comforts of the ways of God. All that perhaps you have yet felt is only a desire to serve God, a wish to lead a more serious life; and you have offered a few prayers, that the Lord would teach you to give up your hearts to him. You are still ignorant, inexperienced, and weak. But if you are really sincere, though you have much to learn, you have nothing to fear.

---

[65] 1 Peter 5:9; James 4:7
[66] 2 Corinthians 2:11
[67] Hebrews 10:39
[68] Isaiah 44:3-5
[69] Psalm 116:16
[70] Psalm 86:11

Your God is one that "despiseth not the day of small things." Your Savior is he that "breaketh not the bruised reed, nor quenches the smoking flax." Like the good Shepherd, he takes especial care of "the lambs: gathering them in his arms, and carrying them in his bosom,"? feeding them with food convenient for them, and leading them as they are able to bear it.[71]

If the prospect of difficulty is too much for the weakness of your faith, look to him who has enabled you to put your hands to the plough; and he will enable you to keep it there without looking back. Remember—he hath said—"I will never leave thee, nor forsake thee." Remember that the feeblest faith will give you a present interest in this and in every promise of his word. And what can you want beside to hold you up, and hold you on to the end? It is the daily exercise of this faith that will strengthen your resolutions, and impart spiritual life to your convictions; while the want of it gives a fearful power to temptations, and leads you to faint in secret prayer, and at last utterly to fall. In such a service—with such a Master—all is full of encouragement. The bands with which you have been "drawn," and which are still cast around you, are "bands of love." Will you not try to have them fastened more firmly? What a subject of praise, that the bonds of sin should be loosed, that you might be cheerfully, and for ever the servants of God![72]

Lastly—*I would say to all, who will hear*—prove that you really did give your heart to God on the day of Confirmation, by giving it to him every day, yea many times a day. And prove the sincerity of this daily dedication, by increasing fear of going back! by lowliness of mind, tenderness of conscience, separation from the spirit and temper of the world, and by resistance to temptation. Be watchful over your words, your tempers, your inclinations, and especially your besetting sins. We do not indeed expect from you the obedience of an Angel; but we must see—the Church of God must see—nay, the world with all their blindness and unwillingness to be convinced, must see, that " you are new creatures, that old things are passed away, and that all things are become new." Thus you will "adorn the doctrine of God your Savior in all things, so that you will "come behind in no gift; waiting for the coming of our Lord Jesus Christ; who shall also confirm you unto the end."[73]

---

[71] Zechariah 4:10; Isaiah 42:3; 40:11

[72] Hebrews 13:5; Hosea 11:4; Psalm 116:16

[73] 2 Corinthians 5:17; Titus 2:10; 1 Corinthians 1:7,8

A PRAYER AFTER CONFIRMATION

O MOST merciful Father, I bless thee that I have been permitted, unworthy as I am, to take upon myself the vows made for me at my baptism. Pardon the wanderings of my heart, and the coldness of my prayers when I was confirmed; and let me not lose the promised blessing.

And now, Lord, I am thy servant; grant that I may be thine for ever. Pity the weakness, folly, and ignorance of my youth: save me from the snares of Satan and of the world, and above all, from the wickedness of my own deceitful heart. Teach me more and more my need of Jesus to be my Savior. Give me faith in him, so that I may know him as "the way, the truth, and the life," and come to him daily for cleansing in his blood, and for strength to love and serve him. Strengthen me, O Lord, with the Holy Ghost, the Comforter. May the Bible be my daily guide. Teach me to pray over it, understand it, and love it. Fill me with a holy fear; and so lead and keep me in thy ways, that I may never go back from thee, but, through the power of thy grace in Christ Jesus, may attain everlasting life.

And now, O Lord, help me to prepare for giving myself up again to thee at the Table of thy dear Son. May I there eat of that bread, and drink of that cup, so that I may remember my Savior, feed upon him by faith with thanksgiving, and be strengthened and refreshed in my soul.

Lord, teach and help me to repent, believe, and live as becomes thy Gospel, for Jesus Christ's sake, Amen.

SGCB Titles for the Young

Solid Ground Christian Books is honored to be able to offer a full dozen uncovered treasure for children and young people.

The Child's Book on the Fall by Thomas H. Gallaudet is a simple and practical exposition of the Fall of man into sin, and his only hope of salvation.

Repentance & Faith: *Explained and Illustrated for the Young* by Charles Walker, is a two in one book introducing children to the difference between true and false faith and repentance.

The Child at Home by John S.C. Abbott is the sequel to his popular book *The Mother at Home.* A must read for children and their parents.

My Brother's Keeper: *Letters to a Younger Brother* by J.W. Alexander contains the actual letters Alexander sent to his ten year old brother.

The Scripture Guide by J.W. Alexander is filled with page after page of information on getting the most from our Bibles. Invaluable!

Feed My Lambs: *Lectures to Children* by John Todd is drawn from actual sermons preached in Philadelphia, PA and Pittsfield, MA to the children of the church, one Sunday each month. A pure gold-mine of instruction.

Heroes of the Reformation by Richard Newton is a unique volume that introduces children and young people to the leading figures and incidents of the Reformation. Spurgeon called him, *"The Prince of preachers to the young."*

Heroes of the Early Church by Richard Newton is the sequel to the above-named volume. The very last book Newton wrote introduces all the leading figures of the early church with lessons to be learned from each figure.

The King's Highway: *Ten Commandments to the Young* by Richard Newton is a volume of Newton's sermons to children. Highly recommended!

The Life of Jesus Christ for the Young by Richard Newton is a double volume set that traces the Gospel from Genesis 3:15 to the Ascension of our Lord and the outpouring of His Spirit on the Day of Pentecost. Excellent!

The Young Lady's Guide by Harvey Newcomb will speak directly to the heart of the young women who desire to serve Christ with all their being.

The Chief End of Man by John Hall is an exposition and application of the first question of the Westminster Shorter Catechism. Full of rich illustrations.

Call us Toll Free at 1-877-666-9469
Send us an e-mail at sgcb@charter.net
Visit us on line at solid-ground-books.com

John Eadie Titles

Solid Ground is delighted to announce that we have republished several volumes by John Eadie, gifted Scottish minister. The following are in print:

Commentary on the Greek Text of Paul's Letter to the Galatians
Part of the classic five-volume set that brought world-wide renown to this humble man, Eadie expounds this letter with passion and precision. In the words of Spurgeon, "This is a most careful attempt to ascertain the meaning of the Apostle by painstaking analysis of his words."

Commentary on the Greek Text of Paul's Letter to the Ephesians
Spurgeon said, "This book is one of prodigious learning and research. The author seems to have read all, in every language, that has been written on the Epistle. It is also a work of independent criticism, and casts much new light upon many passages."

Commentary on the Greek Text of Paul's Letter to the Philippians
Robert Paul Martin wrote, "Everything that John Eadie wrote is pure gold. He was simply the best exegete of his generation. His commentaries on Paul's epistles are valued highly by careful expositors. Solid Ground Christian Books has done a great service by bringing Eadie's works back into print."

Commentary on the Greek Text of Paul's Letter to the Colossians
According to the New Schaff-Herzog Encyclopedia of Religious Knowledge, "These commentaries of John Eadie are marked by candor and clearness as well as by an evangelical unction not common in works of the kind." Spurgeon said, "Very full and reliable. A work of utmost value."

Commentary on the Greek Text of Paul's Letters to the Thessalonians
Published posthumously, this volume completes the series that has been highly acclaimed for more than a century. Invaluable.

Paul the Preacher: A Popular and Practical Exposition of His Discourses and Speeches as Recorded in the Acts of the Apostles
Very rare volume intended for a more popular audience, this volume begins with Saul's conversion and ends with Paul preaching the Gospel of the Kingdom in Rome. It perfectly fills in the gaps in the commentaries. Outstanding work!

DIVINE LOVE: A Series of Doctrinal, Practical and Experimental Discourses
Buried over a hundred years, this volume consists of a dozen complete sermons from Eadie's the pastoral ministry. "John Eadie, the respected nineteenth-century Scottish Secession minister-theologian, takes the reader on an edifying journey through this vital biblical theme." - Ligon Duncan

Lectures on the Bible to the Young for Their Instruction and Excitement
"Though written for the rising generation, these plain addresses are not meant for mere children. Simplicity has, indeed, been aimed at in their style and arrangement, in order to adapt them to a class of young readers whose minds have already enjoyed some previous training and discipline." – Author's Preface

Printed in the United States
54616LVS00002BA/301-318

9 781599 250281